Jesus Never Said Anything New

Matt Rosenberg

Unless otherwise noted, all Scripture quotations are taken from Tree of Life Translation of the Bible. Copyright © 2015 by The Messianic Jewish Family Bible Society.

Scripture quotations marked (CJB) are taken from the Complete Jewish Bible, Copyright © 1998 by David H. Stern. All rights reserved.

Scripture quotations marked (KJV) are taken from the King James Bible. Accessed on Bible Gateway. www.BibleGateway.com.

Scripture quotations marked (NASB) are taken from the New American Standard Bible ® (NASB), copyright © 1960, 1962, 1963, 1968, 1971, 1972, 1973, 1975, 1977, 1995 by The Lockman Foundation. Used by permission. www.Lockman.org.

Sermon To Book
www.sermontobook.com

Jesus Never Said Anything New / Matt Rosenberg
ISBN-13: 978-1-952602-30-6

Prepare for an awakening. In a way I didn't know was possible, *Jesus Never Said Anything New* makes the words of Jesus come more alive. It provides a depth and context that will change the way you read, study, and understand everything He said.

Shawn Hennessey | Senior Pastor
Life Church Green Bay
Chaplain | Green Bay Packers
Green Bay, WI

Jesus is Jewish! Nothing seems so basic, yet nothing seems to be more ignored in seeking to know Jesus as revealed in the four Gospels. With scholarship and wit, Matt unpacks for us this essential facet of knowing Jesus who came as the Jewish Messiah and the Savior of the nations. If you truly want to know Jesus, your time will be well spent reading this book, then slowly reading the Gospels once again.

David McQueen | Lead Pastor
Beltway Park Church
Abilene, TX

In our day and age, far too many followers of Jesus are willing to jettison the very Scriptures that shaped Jesus' own life, teaching, and ministry. I am so thankful for my friend Matt's tenacious commitment to inviting us to the Bible as a unified whole. People of the Messiah—both Jew and Gentile—will benefit from seriously considering what Rabbi Matt has to say in this book.

Aaron Gray | Pastor of Preaching and Vision
Sound City Bible Church
Lynnwood, WA

Rabbi Matt helps put Jesus in His proper first-century Jewish context in a way that is accessible to anyone, no matter where you are in your journey of faith. He unwinds common misunderstandings about Jesus and invites you to make simple application of these newfound perspectives to your life today. Matt's insights are a gift to everyone, and I am grateful that he took the time to share this with the rest of us!

Rabbi Troy Wallace | Vice President
Jewish Voice Ministries International
Phoenix, AZ

As a young lead pastor teaching the Scriptures, I knew I was reading and living out a Jewish book. Yes—it's for all of us—but it is rooted in God's dealings with and promises to his oldest friends. So I began to ask the Lord to provide me friends who could help make his book come as fully alive to my own heart and then to other hearts through a teaching ministry. Rabbi Matt is one of those God has provided me. His book *Jesus Never Said Anything New* is an answer to some of the prayers you've prayed for insight and understanding in the word and ways of God. Matt is well situated to be a bridge builder between those who serve the local church and the Messianic community. Do yourself a favor: take some time, listen to Rabbi Matt, and learn.

Chris Manginelli | Lead Pastor
Mill Creek Foursquare Church
Mill Creek, WA

There is nothing more important to the followers of Yeshua than what He said to us. The context of his message informs us for all parts of our lives. Matt does the important work or restoring the words of Jesus back into their historic and theological context. This helps the reader to understand and affirm the divinity and kingship of the Messiah while uniquely affirming the continuity of the Scriptures.

Rabbi Jacob Rosenberg, PhD | Adat HaTikvah
Deerfield, IL

Rabbi Matt has written what we've all needed to hear. He first demonstrates the key importance of understanding the Jewish context of the words of Yeshua and His early followers. But then, he drills down to what is centrally important—the heart of man and our need to turn to God. Rabbi Matt shows that it's not about legalism, but at the same time, you don't throw out the Jewish roots of the faith with the bathwater. On the contrary, they deliver rich meaning that is enlightening to both Jewish and Gentile believers. So many questions are answered in one book! Yasher Koach!

Rabbi Kevin Solomon | Beth Hallel
Roswell, GA

This book will help both Jewish people and Christians discover the real Jesus—an observant first-century Jew from Israel who correctly taught the essence of Judaism to his people. Thank you, Rabbi Matt, for a book that may seem new but in truth is very old. Everyone seeking truth needs to read this!

Jonathan Bernis | Host
Jewish Voice w/ Jonathan Bernis

For my parents, David and Helene Rosenberg, who introduced me to Yeshua and gave me an unbreakable Jewish identity centered on our Messiah. I love you.

CONTENTS

Foreword by Pastor Tim Ross

I want you to think back to the first story you ever heard about Jesus. Perhaps it was about His amazing miracles, His love and passion for humanity, His horrific death on the cross, or His glorious resurrection from death to life. Do you have one in mind? Good! Do you remember the storyteller ever mentioning the fact that Jesus was Jewish? That He was the fulfillment of the covenant that God made to Abraham, Jacob, Moses, and David?

Do you remember anyone telling you that this Jewish Jesus, Messiah to Jewish people, came to save His people and subsequently every other person that would call on the name of the Lord?

No? Me, either! I know some of you were fortunate enough to be blessed with a Bible teacher who was theologically sound enough to communicate the gospel message of Jesus Christ with an understanding of Jewish history, but for most of us?

Yeah. Not so much.

This is why *Jesus Never Said Anything New* is a must read for anyone with the desire to have context for the things Jesus said.

My friend Matt guides us through the life and words of Jesus so that we can gain clarity with simplicity. Think of him as an interpreter. This book is filled with "all He's trying to say is..." moments that will make you say, "Now I get it!" or "Duh! That's so easy. Why have we made this so hard?"

These are the moments that will allow us to grow in our relationship with Jesus. The more uncomplicated He becomes, the more compelling He becomes. Jesus never did away with the testament of old, because *Jesus Never Said Anything New*!

With this understanding I feel it's imperative for Gentiles (me being one of them) to return "our Bibles" back to the people it was originally written for, the Jewish people.

Only then can we feel how amazing adoption really is, how supernatural engrafting is, how truly amazing God's grace is!

Tim Ross | Lead Pastor
Embassy City Church
Author of *Upset The World*
Irving, TX

INTRODUCTION

Let Joy Reign

As I write this, I sit in Jerusalem during Sukkot, the Feast of Tabernacles.[1] Among the Jewish people, it is known as "the season of our joy."[2] Because of the truth of Scripture, we are constantly in a season of joy, even while the world is going crazy in darkness. That's the paradox in which we live.

My name, *Matthew Asher*, means "God's gift of happiness." I used to joke that my name meant "God's gift to women," but I had to stop saying that once I got married! Truthfully, God could have given up on me a long time ago, but because of His mercy and grace, He never has, and He never will. Simply put, that makes me happy! I believe that the reason I exist is to inspire people to see the faithfulness of God through joy.

I encounter far too many angry followers of Yeshua in this crazy world. If He really is the Messiah, the Son of God, the King of Israel, the image of the invisible God (Colossians 1:15), and if He really did die and rise from the dead to bring us repentance and forgiveness of our sins, then there is great joy to be found!

Perhaps it's time to let that joy engulf all those who believe in Yeshua. In the words of Mikey in the movie *The Goonies*, "Look how far we've come. We've got a chance. ... Down here, it's our time. It's our time down here. That's all over the second we ride up Troy's bucket."[3]

Don't ride up Troy's bucket. Let's let joy reign in our hearts and our minds as we celebrate Yeshua together.

I want to be clear up front—I am not against Christianity, after all Christianity is Judaism for Gentiles. As a Messianic Jew, I am a part of two peoples: Israel and the church. I am Jewish and thus a part of the people of Israel who made a covenant with God at Mt. Sinai. I am a follower of Yeshua, which makes me a part of the body of Messiah (joined with Gentile Christians in what many call the church). I care deeply about both of my "families" and want to see the gap between them filled with Jewish context. To paraphrase one of my heroes, Dr. David H. Stern: proclaiming the gospel without its Jewishness restored is not preaching the full or whole gospel.

I do not believe that Messianic Judaism is the only right way to approach Yeshua. It is, however, important to the faith of any believer in Jesus to understand His Jewishness. Christianity comes from Judaism, not the other way around. The original Jewish disciples had to decide what was required of Gentiles (Acts 15), because Gentiles were turning to the God of Israel but were also not becoming Jews. My goal in writing this book is to help both Jews and Christians understand the historical and Jewish context of Yeshua, His teachings, and rites and celebrations that are considered traditionally "Christian" but are really "Jewish" in their inception. My goal is not for everyone to keep the Torah but for everyone—both Jews and Gentiles—to see the New Testament as a Jewish book, a part of the Hebrew Scriptures. I say often in my preaching to my congregation in

Seattle, "Jews are Jews, Gentiles are Gentiles, and together we are the family of God." Understanding the Jewishness of Jesus enhances the identity of both Jews and Gentiles who identify as His followers. I hope to help you think and see the Scriptures differently while also making you laugh.

Thank you for joining me on this adventure. I pray it is helpful to you and draws you closer to the God of Abraham, Isaac, and Jacob, in the person of Yeshua.

CHAPTER ONE

Yeshua

I attended a Christian college in upstate New York. Throughout my time there, I wore a kippah, which is a traditional Jewish head covering,[4] and tzitzit, the tassels or fringes described in Numbers 15:37–40.[5] Observant Jews typically wear both.

During the first few weeks of my freshman year, several people approached me to share God's offer of salvation through Jesus Christ. Their assumption was that, since I looked so religiously Jewish, I most certainly did not know Jesus. Otherwise, I would've put all that Jewish stuff behind me and become a Christian who looked like them.

Don't worry—I'm a New Yorker living in Seattle, so I know how to hold my own and speak up for myself. Standing out doesn't intimidate me. College was a wonderful experience for me. I met my wife, Laura, as well as my best friends, who are pastors. I grew tremendously in my faith and theology.

Twenty years later, it continues to amaze me that the vast majority of people find it hard to believe that Jews can follow

Jesus while still practicing Judaism centered on the Jewish Messiah.

The Jewishness of Jesus

These days, most people seem to know Jesus was Jewish, but it wasn't so long ago that this fact used to surprise people. I'm an American mix of Jewish (my father's side) and Italian (my mother's side). My Italian Roman-Catholic grandmother once asked me if I knew who the two greatest Italians in history were. I told her I didn't know and asked which two made her list. She said: "Frank Sinatra and Jesus!"

There's no question about Sinatra's heritage—or that he's one of the greatest Italians in history—but I had to gently explain to my grandma that Jesus was not Italian. He never even visited Rome, much less Italy.

It might throw you off, however, to hear that not only was Jesus Jewish, He is still Jewish as He sits at the right hand of the Father. In fact, in His thirty-three years on this earth, He was never referred to as "Jesus." His given name was Yeshua, which literally means "salvation" in Hebrew.[6]

There's nothing wrong with the English name "Jesus," of course. Demons respond to it, just as they respond to His name in any language. And thankfully, our salvation depends on accepting Jesus' sacrificial death on the cross as atonement for our sins, not on getting His name exactly right.

During His time on this earth, Yeshua never spoke English. He spoke Hebrew, Aramaic, and probably some Greek. He lived in the land we know as Israel as an observant Jew and rabbi. He never visited the United States—for one thing, it didn't exist yet. The furthest from home that He traveled was

Egypt.

Yeshua attended synagogue and celebrated Shabbat [Sabbath].[7] As an observant Jew, Yeshua kept all of the commandments required of Him. He celebrated Shabbat weekly, He attended synagogue, He prayed in the Temple in Jerusalem on Jewish holidays (John 10:22–23), He never ate unclean food. His parents, also observant Jews, brought him to Jerusalem to be circumcised on the eighth day, offered the prescribed sacrifice after his mother's days of purification were over, and named him a Jewish name, Yeshua (Luke 2:21–23).

The blonde-haired, blue eyed, clean-shaven, soft white skin of the Jesus in Michelangelo's *Last Judgment*—basically, the Western world view of Jesus—is far removed from Rabbi Yeshua, son of Yosef [Joseph][8] the carpenter from Natzeret [Nazareth] in Eretz Yisrael [Land of Israel].[9]

Some prominent modern rabbis and authors are arguing that Judaism should take Jesus back as a good Jew and rabbi. In his book *Kosher Jesus*, Shmuley Boteach—famously known as Michael Jackson's rabbi—makes the case that Jesus was a good Jew and that everything He taught was in the context of first-century Judaism.

Boteach also asserts that Jesus has been de-Judaized:

> The people who represented him in this way had a vested interest in doing so. They superimposed onto Jesus their own antipathy toward Jews. They ripped a Jewish patriot away from his people. They portrayed his teachings as being hostile to Judaism when, in fact, everything he taught stemmed from the Judaism he practiced.[10]

Judaism for Dummies, a primer for Judaism in layman's terms, calls modern Judaism "completely incompatible with a belief in Jesus as Messiah."[11] But the book also acknowledges that "similarities exist between Jesus' teachings and the rabbinic literature of his time. For example, his emphasis on 'Thou shalt love the Eternal One your God...' and 'love your neighbor as yourself' are totally congruent with rabbinic teachings."[12]

So, which one is it? Is Judaism "completely incompatible" with Jesus, or are His teachings "totally congruent with rabbinic teachings?" It can't be both. What if everything He taught was Jewish and in the context of first-century Judaism? There was nothing new in what Yeshua was teaching that made any of the Jews of His time question whether Yeshua was Jewish or if He was teaching Judaism.

Daniel Boyarin, an orthodox Jewish author and professor at Berkley writes in his book *The Jewish Gospels* that "Jesus' Judaism was a conservative reaction against some radical innovations in the Law stemming from the Pharisees and Scribes of Jerusalem."[13] It's a bit jarring to read that sentence because it is the opposite of how the majority of Christians understand Yeshua's relationship with the Pharisees: Jesus was the radical innovator, and the Pharisees were His legalistic agitators. But, if what Boyarin is stating here is true, it changes how we all understand this important relationship in the Gospels. So, what were the radical innovations of the Pharisees? That's a great question, and we will come back to it later. The point I am making here is, Christians often see Jesus as an innovator who came to leave Judaism behind and start something new called Christianity. Non-messianic Jewish people see Jesus as a good Jew who followed Judaism, and His "followers" were the ones who made Him into "God in flesh" (John 1:14, paraphrased).

One prominent German rabbi in the eighteenth century, Jacob Emden, wrote:[14]

The Nazarene brought about a double kindness in the world. On the one hand, He strengthened the Torah of Moses majestically, as mentioned earlier, and not one of our Sages spoke out more emphatically concerning the immutability of the Torah. And on the other hand, He did much good for the Gentiles.

Another rabbi, from the late nineteenth century, said, "Jesus was a good Jew who did not dream of founding a rival church."[15]

In a *New York Times* article titled, "Jewish Scholars Reassessing Historical Jesus" from 1978, Dr. Pinchas Lapide was asked about Jesus and said:[16]

"We Jews are very proud of our Einsteins, Heinrich Heines and Sigmund Freuds. ...We ought to be much prouder of Jesus. ... Jesus was as faithful to the law as I would hope to be. I even suspect that Jesus was more faithful to the law than I am—and [I] am an Orthodox Jew."

In one of his numerous books about Jesus and the New Testament, he said, "Any Jewish scholar who examines the New Testament will find that Jesus was undoubtedly a Jew—not just a marginal Jew, nor a lukewarm, pro forma Jew, but a true Jew, whose spiritual roots rose out of the prophetic core of Israel's faith."[17]

Norman Cousins, former editor of the *Saturday Review*, wrote:[18][19]

There is every reason for Judaism to lose its reluctance toward Jesus. His own towering spiritual presence is a projection of Judaism, not a repudiation of it. Jesus is not to be taxed for the un-Christian ideas and acts of those who have spoken in his name. Jesus never repudiated Judaism. He was proud to be a Jew, yet he did not confine himself to Judaism. He did not believe in spiritual exclusivity for either Jew or Gentile. He asserted the Jewish heritage and sought to preserve and exalt its values, but he did it within a universal context. No other figure—spiritual, philosophical, political or intellectual—has had a greater impact on human history.

Maimonides, recognized as one of the most important rabbis in Jewish history, said:[20]

All these matters which refer to Jesus of Nazareth ... only served to make the way free for the King Messiah and to prepare the whole world for the worship of God with a united heart, as it is written: *"Yea, at that time I will change the speech of the peoples to a pure speech, that all of them may call on the name of the LORD and serve him with one accord"* (Zeph. 3:9). In this way the messianic hope, the Torah, and the commandments have become a widespread heritage of faith—among the inhabitants of the far islands and among many nations, uncircumcised in heart and flesh."

Jewish Christian Abram Poljak wrote in his 1938 book, *The Cross in the Star of David*: [21]

Never has the Jewish people been so near to the idea of the Kingship of Jesus. But we must not demand too much at once ... [for] the Jewish people as a whole will not at once accept Jesus as their Messiah; but they will first cease to condemn Him. Then they will begin to think about Him, recognize Him as their brother, their teacher, and at last acknowledge Him as a prophet and "the Jew who is the central figure."

Perhaps, with the growth we've seen of Messianic Judaism over the last century, we are seeing this come true. The first step to my people accepting Yeshua as the Messiah is understanding Him as a Jew who spoke Hebrew, because it is crucial to understanding Yeshua, the Gospels, and the New Testament as part of the Jewish canon of Scripture.

At the same time, there is a deeply engrained idea that Jesus, or for many, Paul, left Judaism behind and that to go back to Judaism is to move backwards in revelation. Many people believe that Paul abrogated, or did away with, the Torah—which is a great slander.

The Torah is the first five books of the Bible, known as the Books of Moses. In much of Christian theology, the law of Moses (the Torah) is believed to be abrogated (done away with) in light of new revelation of Jesus. My contention is that the law of Moses is not done away with for Jewish people. There are specific commandments for the Jewish people, like circumcision, the sabbath, the feast of the Lord, and not eating unclean food, that Jesus and the New Testament never undo. Rather, the writers of the New Testament, mainly Paul, tried to show that Gentiles are not obligated to do all the same things.

In truth, Gentiles never were obligated. When a Gentile says, "I am set free from the law," they usually mean they can eat whatever they want. In fact, Gentiles could always eat whatever they wanted. If one was never forbidden from something, you cannot be set free from it. Some laws that never were given to Gentiles still remain for Jews. At times, Judaism added rules and called their added rules "Torah," or the law of Moses. This is where the confusion comes in. Their added rules are not Torah and yet they refer to it as Torah. For Messianic Jews like me, the Torah only includes the commandments found in the actual five Books of Moses. It's the difference between oral Torah and written Torah.

Paul accomplished so much for the kingdom of God, at great personal risk, and so many people misunderstand him, thinking he taught the exact opposite of what he actually taught. So many Christians believe he taught the end of the law, when in reality he taught no such thing. How frustrating it would be to have someone listen to a sermon I preached and come away believing I said the opposite of what I actually said!

Preaching the Jewish Messiah
to Jews and Gentiles

In the early 1990s, practically every teen in every church youth group had a bracelet bearing the acronym W.W.J.D? which stood for "What Would Jesus Do?" I had a bracelet like that, and my dad asked me what it meant. When I explained, he asked me a question. That's a very Jewish thing to do, to answer a question with a question.

"Do you know what the answer to that question really is?" my dad asked me. "He would go to synagogue!"

Simple, right? So often, without giving it much thought, the majority of people who believe in Jesus remove His Jewishness and His committed practice of His Jewish faith.

For me, it all goes back to my bar mitzvah and the haftarah[22]—a reading from the Prophets—from the book of Amos, the place where I found my calling from God at the age of thirteen:

> "In that day I will raise up David's fallen sukkah.[23] I will restore its breaches, raise up its ruins, and rebuild it as in days of old—so they may possess the remnant of Edom and all the nations called by My Name." It is a declaration of ADONAI, the One who will do this.
>
> —Amos 9:11–12

Bar mitzvah means "son of the commandments" and it is a rite of passage, traditionally at thirteen, when a young man reads from the Torah in Hebrew at synagogue for the first time.[24] According to tradition, there are set readings for every Saturday of the year, called Torah portions. Because of the date of my bar mitzvah, which is connected to my birthday, Leviticus 18–19 as well as Amos 9:7–15 became life scriptures, as they were the set reading for the day of my bar mitzvah. In Judaism, you generally refer to the selected portions of the Bible from your bar mitzvah—bat mitzvah for girls—as "my Torah portion."

At thirteen years old—and for most of my adult life—I assumed these verses were about God's call on my life to preach the gospel to my Jewish people. Like Paul, my burden is for my own people (Romans 9:1–5) and to see a revival of Jewish people returning to the God of our fathers through our Messiah Yeshua. It's part of my design and what makes my heart beat.

As I've gotten older, and probably around the start of my second decade in ministry, God's desire to call both Jews and Gentiles back to Himself began to resonate with me. What would it look like for a Messianic synagogue to preach the gospel in a Jewish context? What if both Gentiles and Jews responded to the preaching of the continuity of the Tanakh[25]— the Hebrew Bible—and the New Testament?

What if Gentiles, some of whom have been disenfranchised and disappointed by the church, might respond to the Jewishness of Jesus and His disciples? This isn't to say that Gentiles would become Jews, but that they could become more historically minded and treat the New Testament as a Jewish book. What would that look like?

In the Messianic movement and on the internet, people have

made the word Gentile a bad word. This may be partially influenced by Judaism and the pejorative use of the word *goy*, which refers to a non-Jewish person, in conversation and in writing.[26] But the word Gentile simply means "nation,"[27] and God's heart has certainly always been for the nations. God's covenant with Abraham included the idea that in the Jewish people "all the families of the earth will be blessed" (Genesis 12:3).

I initially thought I was called to be an apostle to the Jewish people, like Peter. Now I wrestle with the idea that I might be called to be an apostle to the Gentiles, like Paul. Don't get me wrong—I'm not comparing myself to Peter and Paul, and I certainly don't regard myself as an apostle. I'm not interested in a false sense of my own importance. It's about the direction in which God is drawing my heart.

Maybe all believers in Yeshua are called to be a combination of both. Maybe every congregation on the planet that calls on the name of Yeshua is supposed to have both Jews and Gentiles as members.

For me, to raise the fallen sukkah, or shelter, of David is a calling to restore Judaism and the Jewish people back to Yeshua's faith. "And all the nations called by My Name" (Amos 9:12) represents God's desire to call all the nations back to Himself. It is the privilege of my life to be invited by God into this Great Commission, to preach and teach both Jews and Gentiles about the history of redemption and the work the Holy Spirit is doing in this post-modern age.

CHAPTER TWO

Setting the Stage

I hate to break it to you, but Jesus never said anything new.

When the gospel is preached, Jesus is often portrayed as an innovator. And if it's not Jesus who's given innovator status, it's Paul. People tend to think that Judaism fulfilled the things of Scripture and was then abandoned by Jesus and Paul, who then created Christianity.

Jesus was not an innovator. At the very least, He was a reformer. If He was not a reformer, then He was a restorer.

Andy Stanley, in his book *Irresistible: Reclaiming the New That Jesus Unleashed on the World*, says:[28]

> Jesus steps into history and introduces something new. He didn't come to Jerusalem offering a new version of an old thing or an update to an existing thing. He didn't come to make something better. Jesus was sent by the Father to introduce something entirely new.

I agree with Andy that Jesus did not come offering a new version of Judaism—or, as he says later in his book, that Christianity was not "version 2.0 of Judaism."[29] But Jesus did not come to start "something entirely new," either. He came to take the Jewish people back to something older. Like all of the prophets before him, He came to correct.

Reformed (not a follower of Jesus) Rabbi Hyman G. Enelow said (emphasis added):[30]

> Jesus was not only born a Jew, but conscious of his Jewish descent. Jesus realized the spiritual distinction of the Jewish people and regarded himself as sent to teach and help his people. Jesus, like other teachers, **severely criticized his people for their spiritual shortcomings, seeking to correct them, but at the same time he loved and pitied them.** His whole ministry was saturated with love for his people, and loyalty to it.

"This is totally brand new and really different from everything we know about the Torah and observe in Judaism," said no one to any of the teachings of Yeshua recorded in the Gospels. What made leaders angry and intrigued His average listener about Yeshua was the authority with which He spoke, not the content of what He taught.

Andy Stanley is right. He didn't come to Jerusalem offering a new version of an old thing or an update to an existing thing. Yeshua came to correct, like all the prophets before Him, the places where Israel and its rabbis had strayed from the original message of the Torah. It's not new. It's old. Much older than first-century, Second Temple Judaism. Old, as in when Yeshua wrote it and gave it to Moses (Exodus 31:18). This is the dilemma in turning the Torah into a moral code, a list of right and wrong. As Brennan Manning wrote in *The Signature of Jesus*, "We cushion the risk and remove the danger of discipleship by drawing up a list of moral rules that give us security instead of holy insecurity."[31] When the Torah is reduced to rule-keeping, it misses the heart behind the Torah itself: loving God and loving people.

Yeshua's frustration with the Pharisees and Sadducees in the Gospels came down to authority. Did they have authority, or, as God, did He? It was the conversation with the Pharisees about Abraham (John 8:12–59). How could He know Abraham when He wasn't even fifty years old? Yeshua responded with, "before Abraham was I am" (John 8:58). They got angry. Because not only was He saying, "I have more authority than you," but He was also saying "I am the God of Abraham, Isaac, and Jacob!" It wasn't new. It just made them angry. God becoming a man was not new, either. See every time the angel of the Lord appeared and someone worshiped Him.

I'm sure some of you are already saying to yourselves, "I'm pretty sure Jesus said some new stuff," and are flipping through your Bibles in search of evidence. I understand why you're skeptical, and that's why I've tested this concept on a lot of people, including various pastors and Messianic rabbis. All have provided positive feedback regarding what I'm going to show you.

Jesus didn't come to earth to introduce new ideas. In fact, the content of His teachings was the same as all the other first-century rabbis who were speaking from the Hebrew Scriptures.

Here are some points to consider as we begin our adventure together. These will be further developed over the course of the book.

The Physical Portrayal of Jesus

When you see a painting or an illustration of Jesus, He's usually a white dude with super-soft skin and hair. He definitely moisturizes and uses conditioner. Even as a Jewish believer, I picture Yeshua as a white man with long brown hair wearing a white robe and a purple sash. From Italian Renaissance masterpieces to modern-day Catholic prayer cards, it's perhaps the most common portrayal of Him in Western art.

A light-hearted example of this is: in Leonardo da Vinci's *Last Supper*, everybody is eating fish at the table. It can be presumed that Leonardo da Vinci was Catholic (he lived just before the Protestant Reformation) and was accustomed to eating fish on Fridays. Perhaps he assumed that Jesus and His disciples were eating fish because Catholics ate fish on Friday.

Some believe the food that Leonardo painted on the plates is eel.[32] However, we must note that Jesus did not eat eel, because eel is not kosher. Additionally, in Exodus 12:8–9, the Torah commands Jewish people to eat lamb on Passover:

> *That same night they are to eat the meat roasted over the fire, along with bitter herbs, and bread made without yeast. Do not eat the meat raw or boiled in water, but roast it over a fire—with the head, legs and internal organs.*

So, Leonardo's depiction of a Passover meal becomes at best the wrong meat—fish. Or at worst, not a kosher (clean) meat—eel. This, rather than lamb, which certainly is what they ate according to the commandment for Passover in Exodus.

My point is: Jesus was often portrayed as something other than Jewish, and that portrayal is dominant in people's minds today.

It may surprise you to know that Jesus never self-identified as a Christian, or "Christ-follower." First, He was Jewish. Second, He was not a Christ-follower—He was the Christ, the Messiah, the Anointed One. Everyone else followed *Him*, so He wouldn't have identified as a Christian.

Jesus and the Prophets

Jesus spoke from all three parts of the Hebrew Bible—the Torah, the Prophets, and the Writings—and in many cases from Jewish tradition. When He spoke, He spoke like the Jewish prophets who came before Him: Amos, Zechariah, Jeremiah, Isaiah, Ezekiel, Zephaniah, and all the rest who came on the scene when the people of Israel needed to be corrected, when they needed to repent and turn back to God.

Everything the prophets did was saturated in the Hebrew Scriptures. The same was true for Yeshua. He was born in Bethlehem, was raised speaking Hebrew, and went to Jerusalem for all the holy days. The Hebrew Scriptures were His life.

So Many Rules

There have always been people who take the things of Scripture and lead people away from God through their wrong interpretation of Scripture. In Jesus' day, there were people in every Jewish faction with the right heart and right motives. There were also people in every Jewish faction with the wrong heart and wrong motives. It's easy to blame everything on the Pharisees as though they were the most evil of people, but in truth, they were not. They were people, and like all people, they struggled with legalism.

We want to know what rules we need to follow so God will

bless us. We want to be given the rules and follow them. We're even okay with being punished for breaking the rules, as long as we know what the rules are. I am the second-born in my family, which means I was born to break the rules. The rules were made for my older brother, Jake, and my little brother, Avi, has no rules. That's how it plays out in a family with three boys.

So, how many commandments are there in the Torah? According to Maimonides, the Jewish philosopher from the twelfth and thirteenth centuries, there are 613.[33] These commandments include things you should do and things you shouldn't do.

In reality, there are a lot more than 613 things we should and shouldn't do. God gave us His commandments so that we would wrestle in our daily lives with who He is and who we are in comparison to Him. They're supposed to bring us back to Him, to make us aware of our sin and encourage us to repent, but too often, we make the rules our god. The difficulty with the number 613 is that in the counting of the commandments, not every "commandment" is actually from the Torah. Many are added in the oral Torah and are not found in the written Torah. More on this later.

The Authority of Yeshua

The simple, yet absolutely crucial, difference between Yeshua and the other first-century rabbis was that they spoke their opinions and He spoke with authority. Remember, the content of His teachings was similar to theirs because they were using the same text. They were all arguing the Hebrew Scriptures.

I love this quote from A. W. Tozer: "Jesus never uttered

opinions."[34] Jesus never did what we often do in Judaism: "Well, Rabbi Hillel says this, and Rabbi Shemai says this, and Rabbi Joshua says this, so choose which interpretation is right for you." Nope, Jesus came on the scene and said, "Here's what I meant when I wrote it."

Do you understand the difference? When you read through the Gospels, you'll notice that no one ever responded to Yeshua with, "Wow, we've never heard this before. This is completely brand new." Instead, they were impressed by the authority with which He spoke. Consider Mark 1:22: "And they were astounded at His teaching, for He was teaching them as one having authority and not as the Torah scholars."

This isn't to say the Torah scholars were wrong or legalistic or had no idea what they were talking about. People were amazed that Yeshua spoke with the authority of the One who had authored the Torah to begin with.

Being amazed by Yeshua's authority, however, doesn't automatically mean that they were happy about it. Some people loved it, and other people hated it. More specifically, it seems in the Gospels that regular people loved him and *some* of the leaders did not.

Like in Mark 1:27, "They were all so amazed that they asked among themselves, 'What is this? A new teaching with authority! He commands even the unclean spirits, and they obey Him!'"

You might be thinking "Wait, it says, 'new teaching,' and the title of this book is *Jesus Never Said Anything New.*" But the newness had to do with the authority He walked in, not in the content He was teaching. Only God could command demons, and if He was commanding demons to leave, then He was equating Himself with God, which was the issue for many leaders. Not what He taught, but rather who He was and what authority He operated under. "So for this reason the Judean leaders kept trying even harder to kill Him—because He was not only breaking Shabbat, but also calling God His own Father, making Himself equal with God" (John 5:18). He didn't break the Sabbath—that was an accusation (we deal with that later)—but they were mad that He was "making Himself equal with God."

He wasn't saying anything new. Take, for example, Matthew 5:27–28: "You have heard that it was said, 'You shall not commit adultery.' But I tell you that everyone who looks upon a woman to lust after her has already committed adultery with her in his heart." Any Jew listening to Him would have recognized the commandments from Exodus 20 not to commit adultery and not to covet your neighbor's wife. They would have understood that lusting after a woman in their mind was a form of adultery.

But it's one thing when a rabbi or a pastor tells you not to do something. It's another thing when God shows up in the flesh to remind you that He meant what He said.

God in the Flesh

John 1:1–3 tells us, "In the beginning was the Word. The Word was with God, and the Word was God. He was with God in the beginning. All things were made through Him, and apart from Him nothing was made that has come into being."

Jesus is God's Word in the flesh. When He spoke, He didn't speak exactly like the other prophets who came before Him. He spoke with the authority of God because He is what Paul calls "the image of the invisible God," (Colossians 1:15). For us, this means that any time God shows up in the image of a man, it's Yeshua—technically, a pre-incarnate Yeshua.

Throughout Scripture, neither God the Father nor God the Holy Spirit had an image aside from the person of Yeshua. When Abraham had a meal with God, it was Yeshua (Genesis 18). When Jacob saw a man standing at the top of the stairway to heaven, it was Yeshua (Genesis 28). When Daniel was in the lion's den and a man showed up to rescue him, that was Yeshua (Daniel 6).

Every time a person shows up in Scripture and is referred to as *yud-hey-vav-hey* (or Yahweh),[3536] it's Yeshua. It always has been, and it always will be.

What about angels showing up?

The Leaders Were Afraid to Lose Power

Jesus began His public ministry at the age of thirty (Luke 3:23). His followers called Him "Rabbi," which means "teacher." They listened to Him and gave up everything to follow Him. Giant crowds gathered to hear Him teach.

The Pharisees weren't upset with Him because of His teachings—they were afraid they would lose power. If Jesus really was the king, He was going to lead a revolt, and if He led a revolt, Rome would step in and have them all killed. It wasn't necessarily that the Pharisees were evil. Rather, they saw Yeshua as a threat to their power as religious leaders and to their own safety and the safety of the Jewish people.

Yeshua's Words Start to Make More Sense

In John 2, John paused in recounting the story of Yeshua and His ministry to tell us this: "So after He was raised from the dead, His disciples remembered that He was talking about this. Then they believed the Scripture and the word that Yeshua had spoken" (John 2:22).

This happens in several places in Scripture—in the Gospels, as well as in the book of Acts after Yeshua had risen from the dead, spent forty days on the earth in His resurrection body, ascended into heaven, and given His Spirit on Shavuot [Pentecost].[37] After all of these things, His disciples essentially said, "Oh! Now we get it!"

Going back to John 2, Yeshua had just finished flipping the tables of the moneychangers and driving out the overpriced sacrificial animals they were peddling. The Pharisees demanded Yeshua give them a sign to prove He had the authority to do this. "'Destroy this Temple,' Yeshua answered them, 'and in three days I will raise it up'" (John 2:19).

The Pharisees were like, "What? It took a long time to build this temple," but John clarified that Yeshua was talking about His body, because He was going to die and be resurrected. It wasn't until after these things happened that the disciples remembered what Yeshua said. Then, they believed the Scripture.

The disciples weren't impressed by Yeshua's teaching because it was anything new. No, they were astonished at who He was. Once they were given the Holy Spirit, their understanding of who Yeshua was brought them back to Scripture.

I imagine the disciples getting together and having amazing conversations:

"Remember when He cursed that fig tree and it withered and died (Mark 11:12–25)? That's similar to what's said in Ezekiel (Ezekiel 15)."

"Or how about the suffering servant prophesied by Isaiah (Isaiah 53)? His death seems to have fulfilled that prophecy."

"And remember when He raised those kids from the dead (Mark 5:21–43, Luke 7:11–17), or when He raised Lazarus from the dead (John 11:1–44)? Incredible!"

They walked with Yeshua for three years, and during that time, they understood next to nothing of what He said. After He rose from the dead and the Holy Spirit was given to them on Shavuot [Pentecost], they finally began to understand.

We've all had that moment where we're in a conversation and someone says something we don't quite get. Later, it clicks, and we understand what everyone else was talking about. In the movie, *Honey, I Shrunk The Kids,* Russ rescues Amy by giving her mouth-to-mouth. Her brother, Nick asks, "Where did you learn artificial respiration?" Russ replies, "French class, kid." It's not until the very end of the movie that Nick says, "Now I get it! French class! Ha!"[38] That's exactly what happened to the disciples.

Yeshua's Reason for Coming

In Matthew 5, Jesus preached the Beatitudes to the crowds that had followed Him: "Blessed are the poor in spirit, for theirs is the kingdom of heaven," and so forth (Matthew 5:3). All these concepts had been stated previously in the Torah and the Prophets. Like the prophets who came before Him, Jesus added some correction to what Israel was currently doing and exhorted them to turn back to God. In Matthew 5:17–20, He said:

> *Do not think that I came to abolish the Torah or the Prophets! I did not come to abolish, but to fulfill. Amen, I tell you, until heaven and earth pass away, not the smallest letter or serif shall ever pass away from the Torah until all things come to pass. Therefore, whoever breaks one of the least of these commandments, and teaches others the same, shall be*

*called least in the kingdom of heaven. But whoever keeps
and teaches them, this one shall be called great in the kingdom of heaven. For I tell you that unless your righteousness
exceeds that of the Pharisees and Torah scholars, you shall
never enter the kingdom of heaven!*

The Torah and Prophets Fulfilled

Now, imagine there were Pharisees and Torah scholars sitting there among the crowds, listening to Yeshua. "Unless
you're more righteous than these guys," Yeshua was telling the
people, "you won't enter the kingdom of heaven."

The Pharisees were regarded as the most righteous of the
Jewish people because of how they kept the Torah. Today, most
people see the Pharisees as Yeshua's adversaries because of the
arguments they had with Him in the Gospels. A small group of
Pharisees were very opposed to Yeshua, but they didn't represent all the Pharisees. Some even became His followers, such
as Nicodemus, Joseph of Arimathea, and later, of course, Paul.
There are even Pharisees who follow Yeshua in attendance at
the Jerusalem council with the apostles, as described in Acts
15.

According to some counts, there were about six thousand
Pharisees in Yeshua's day.[39] Being a Pharisee was a lot like belonging to a political party today, like being a Democrat or a
Republican. If you were a Pharisee, you believed certain things,
you taught certain things, and you lived a certain way. In comparison to the Sadducees—who tended to be very wealthy—the
Pharisees were the upstart, reformation-type party.

Without an understanding of Second Temple Judaism and
first-century Israel,[40] it's easy to see the Pharisees as the bad
guys. The Second Temple period is the time when the Second

Temple stood in Jerusalem. From the times of Ezra and Nehemiah in the Bible to its destruction by the Romans in A.D. 70., this Temple replaced Solomon's (First) Temple. It was during this period of around five hundred years that Pharisaic Judaism developed—from the exile in Babylon to the Jewish people's return through Roman rule in the first century. Jesus and His disciples lived at the end of this period.

Among the Pharisees was a group that followed Yeshua around and asked questions. Many of their questions came from the right place, but often in the Gospels, the writers were making the point that Yeshua had some serious disagreements with these specific leaders. You see in the text that these leaders weren't asking because they truly wanted to know the answers; they wanted to see if they could trip Him up.

What they didn't anticipate was that they were dealing with the God of Israel. Every time they tried to trip up Yeshua, they walked away from the conversation looking like fools. This doesn't mean that Judaism, the Jewish people, and everything God did through Scripture were nullified because these guys had bad attitudes. Yeshua came to correct their attitudes.

It bears repeating that Jesus didn't come to do away with anything. He was very clear about this: "Do not think that I came to abolish the Torah or the Prophets! I did not come to abolish, but to fulfill" (Matthew 5:17). The opposite is typically taught and believed: the Pharisees represented Judaism, and Jesus something new:[41]

> The Pharisees sought to convert other Jews to their way of thinking about God and the Torah, a way of thinking that incorporated seeming changes in the written Torah's practices that were mandated by what the Pharisees called "the tradition of the Elders." The justification of these reforms in

the name of an oral Torah, a tradition passed down by the Elders from Sinai on, would have been experienced by many traditional Jews as a radical change, especially when it involved changing the traditional ways that they and their ancestors had kept the Torah immemorial. At least some of these pharisaic innovations may very well have represented changes in religious practice that took place during the Babylonian Exile, while the Jews who remained "in the land" continued their ancient practices. It is quite plausible, therefore, that other Jews, such as the Galilean Jesus, would reject angrily such ideas as an affront to the Torah and as sacrilege. Jesus' Judaism was a conservative reaction against some radical innovations in the Law stemming from the Pharisees and Scribes of Jerusalem.

Some people interpret the word "fulfill" as meaning that since Jesus fulfilled the Torah and the Prophets, they no longer apply today. Based on the rest of that verse, however, that interpretation doesn't make any sense.

What does it mean for Yeshua to come and fulfill these things? It means He came with the authority from heaven to speak into the nation of Israel as a prophet and say, "What you are thinking is wrong in some cases, and I'm here to correct that."

Judging Prematurely

Deuteronomy 13 and 18 say that when someone shows up, speaking and doing things in the name of God, you're supposed to listen first. After they perform miracles and signs and after you test the things they say to see if they come true, then you can pass judgment on them.

This small group of Pharisees did the opposite. They passed judgment on Yeshua first, condemning Him and putting Him to death. This fact doesn't place blame for Yeshua's death on the Jewish people. He came to offer Himself as a sacrifice. There was no scenario that didn't involve His death. That was the whole point.

Yeshua came to fulfill the Scriptures of the Passover Lamb and of Yom Kippur, the Day of Atonement.[42] The sacrifices made in the Temple brought forgiveness of sin, but when the people inevitably sinned again, they had to sacrifice again. Through the blood of Yeshua, our sin is permanently atoned for and forgiven.

Prophecy and Riddles

I like the way the King James Version phrases Matthew 5:18: "For verily I say unto you, till heaven and earth pass, one jot or one tittle shall in no wise pass from the law, till all be fulfilled." In Hebrew, a jot or a tittle would be like a yod, which is a small Hebrew letter that looks similar to an apostrophe.[43] Not even the smallest yod in God's Word will pass away until all things come to pass.

Even two thousand years later, all things have still not come to pass because Yeshua promised He would come back. That and other promises are yet unfulfilled. Since all things have not yet come to pass, nothing is gone. Nothing is even new.

It's funny how Yeshua can be so confusing. He talked about the old as if it were new, and He talked about the new as if it were old. He spoke in riddles, and He spoke in stories. When you read through the Gospels, everyone—His disciples, the people, the Pharisees, and the Torah scholars—walked away from Him going, "What?"

At the same time, they were impressed by the authority with which He spoke. They were like, "I can tell this guy is on to something, but I have no idea what He's saying."

The Pharisees and Hypocrisy

Remember, Yeshua emphasized that a person could not enter the kingdom of heaven unless their righteousness was greater than that of the Pharisees and the Torah scholars (Matthew 5:20). This is important to keep in mind given the numerous occasions on which He condemned the Pharisees.

> *Woe to you, Torah scholars and Pharisees, hypocrites! For you are like whitewashed tombs, which look beautiful on the outside but inside are full of dead men's bones and everything unclean. In the same way, you appear righteous to men on the outside, but are full of hypocrisy and lawlessness.*
> *—Matthew 23:27–28*

Yeshua was not praising the Pharisees for their righteousness. He was warning the people that some of their religious leaders were hypocrites, and that they had better be more righteous than those hypocrites. That continues to be a problem in our world today. People tell you what you need to do to live righteously, but their example is left wanting, because at the end of the day, We're all fallen human beings.

Yeshua knows all this; He knows you're a hypocrite. And honestly, acknowledging that we're all hypocrites is the best place to start. You can't live a righteous life on your own. That's not a New Testament idea, by the way, that you can't do this on your own. No, the Jewish people have known that all along.

At the same time, Yeshua's goal wasn't necessarily to make people compare themselves to the Pharisees. He wanted them to acknowledge who God is and allow Him to speak through His Scriptures.

God Is the Same

When I was in high school, I took an art class, and I shared a table with my friend Hannah. She was an atheist Jew, and I'm a Jew who believes in Jesus. We were quite the pair.

One day, the two of us were discussing Passover. Hannah asked me what my family did to celebrate the holiday since we believed in Jesus. "Well, Jesus fulfills a lot of things related to Passover, so we still do all the normal stuff," I replied. "The Passover Lamb is Yeshua, and He lifted the cup of redemption. After the meal, He made a new covenant with Israel."

Hannah thought that was interesting, so I asked her how she and her family celebrated Passover since they were atheists. "Oh, we just take God out of it," she said. "We just celebrate it as the triumph of the Jewish people."

I was aghast. "You know the Torah says not to do that, right? The Torah may not be clear as to whether or not to include Jesus in the celebration of the Passover, but it definitely says not to take God out of the holidays and celebrations He instituted."

And yet, we do that all the time. We feel like it doesn't matter what Scripture says because our traditions are more important.

For example, my congregation sang "Amazing Grace" during our Torah procession. I felt a disturbance in the Force in that moment as I sensed Messianic rabbis all over the country being disappointed with me. Many Messianic synagogues distance themselves from Christian songs and terminology in favor of Messianic Jewish songs and Jewish terminology. Some of my contemporaries would be disturbed by our congregation singing a hymn. Plenty of others would not be disturbed at all. But why wouldn't we sing a song like that as we escorted our new Torah scroll to its proper place in our synagogue? We're celebrating the amazing grace God has given to us, and it's not only found in the New Testament.

There's not an angry God in the Old Testament and then nice-guy Jesus in the New Testament. That's not how it works. God is the same yesterday, today, and forever (Hebrews 13:8). He has always shown grace to His people, and He has always provided a Savior, all the way back to when He sent Moses as a deliverer to free His people from Egypt.

Yeshua, however, was different because He spoke with authority as God, because He is God. That's what frustrated the religious leaders and the Pharisees. The fact that He equated Himself with God made them angry, but that didn't mean the concept of a savior was new.

Prophecies Fulfilled

In light of the New Testament, it makes sense that you can work backwards and see that Jesus has fulfilled some of the prophecies from the Old Testament. Consider Psalm 110:1: "ADONAI declares to my Lord: 'Sit at My right hand until I make your enemies a footstool for Your feet.'" That's exactly what's happening now. Jesus has ascended to sit at the right hand of God, and He will remain there until it's time for Him to return (Hebrews 1:3).

The pieces are in there; many just refuse to see them. I can't tell you how many Jewish people I've met who don't believe in Jesus, and hate that I believe in Him, but have never read the New Testament. And I can't tell you how many Christians I've met who have never read the Old Testament because "all they need is the New Testament."

We need to realize that if we want the whole counsel of God, it starts with reading all of Scripture. I recommend using a Bible reading plan that does not start in Genesis and go straight through all the way to Revelation.[44] For one thing, most people give up when they get to Leviticus. More importantly, the Bible is not in chronological order.

The Bible is unlike any other book. It's made up of multiple books, and some of them tell the same stories. Unless you do some work, you don't realize which pieces fit where. It's like a puzzle. Everything has to fit together, and it takes study and understanding.

A New Command

When I say Jesus never said anything new, people ask, "Didn't Jesus use the word *new*?" In fact, He did:

I give you a new commandment, that you love one another. Just as I have loved you, so also you must love one another. By this all will know that you are My disciples, if you have love for one another.
—John 13:34–35

Andy Stanley calls this "new" commandment the platinum rule that trumps the golden rule. His idea being that Jesus took all of the commandments and reduced them from His two greatest to one, and the one that is new is all about how He loved

His disciples. As in, face to face and in the flesh. In the Greek, John clearly used the word *new*. So, how could I be saying He never said anything new if He clearly and quite literally said "a new commandment"?

John continued:

> *Peter said to Him, "Master, why can't I follow You now? I'll lay down my life for You!" Yeshua answers, "Will you lay down your life for Me? Amen, amen I tell you, before the rooster crows, you will deny Me three times!"*
>
> *—John 13:37–38*

Yeshua told Peter he would die just like Him before Yeshua had even died. In the next chapter:

> *Yeshua answered and said to him, "If anyone loves Me, he will keep My word. My Father will love him, and We will come to him and make Our dwelling with him. He who does not love Me does not keep My words. And the word you hear is not Mine, but the Father's who sent Me. These things I have spoken to you while dwelling with you. But the Helper, the Ruach ha-Kodesh [Holy Spirit] whom the Father will send in My name, will teach you everything and remind you of everything that I said to you."*
>
> *—John 14:23–26*

Again, Yeshua is God, and God gave the Jewish people commandments. Here, Yeshua gave His disciples another commandment that included, "If you love me, keep my commandments." God had said that before, in Exodus 20:6: "…showing lovingkindness to the thousands of generations of those who love Me and keep My mitzvot." Loving God and keeping His commandments have always gone together. It's not new.

So, why did Jesus use the word "new"? Back to John 14:26: "But the Helper, the Ruach ha-Kodesh [Holy Spirit] whom the Father will send in My name, will teach you everything and remind you of everything that I said to you." Even though they walked with, ate with, sat with, shared rooms with, celebrated holy days with, and were able to look at Jesus face to face, they still would need the Holy Spirit to explain everything to them, and the Holy Spirit didn't come in fullness for the disciples until fifty days after Jesus' resurrection.

This day is called Shavout, first fruits, and according to Leviticus 23:15, it falls fifty days after Passover. It was then, fifty days later, that they began to understand all that Yeshua had taught them. And it is in the telling of the book of Acts—called the Acts of the Apostles because it was what they did after the Resurrection—that much of what we are talking about is fleshed out.

In context, Jesus' use of *new* had to do with their experience, but it wasn't new information. It wasn't a new commandment, as in one they had never heard before. It was new in the sense that their personal relationship with Yeshua would change how they understood everything. Not new, but a reinterpretation of what they thought they already knew.

It goes back to Yeshua's authority. His content was not any different than some of His contemporary rabbis', but what set Him apart was that He spoke like God and in fact, was God, which means He didn't speak in human opinion. He spoke as the author of the Torah, the God who spoke through the prophets and the God who now came to earth as a man to bring His people back to Himself.

This idea of God calling the Jewish people to return to Him

is all over the Hebrew Scriptures. Zechariah, Amos, Isaiah, Nahum, Jeremiah, Daniel, and others all have variations of Malachi 3:7: "'From the days of your ancestors you have turned aside from My statutes, and have not kept them. Return to Me, and I will return to you,' says ADONAI-Tzva'ot." It's like God saying, "You aren't keeping the commandments right. Return to me and I will show you how." Yeshua did the same thing in the New Covenant. It's not really new, as in never heard of before, but it was new in the sense that God kept making covenants with the Jewish people and the additions to the covenants were fulfillments of things promised in surprising ways.

New Covenant is an interesting term because every covenant God made was new at the time it was given. God made several covenants, and each one was new, but it never negated the previous. It started with Abraham and a promise of relationship and land. The covenant continued with Isaac, Jacob, and Jacob's twelve sons who become the nation of Israel, the Jewish people. God made covenant with Moses and David and, ultimately, through Yeshua. Each one new. We will come back to the term *New Covenant* later, when we talk about communion in its Jewish context.

Again, when the Torah is reduced to rule keeping, it misses the heart behind the Torah itself: loving God and loving people. If you're not keeping commandments out of love, you aren't keeping them, as they say on every episode of *The Bachelorette*, for the right reasons.

The danger of turning Jesus into an innovator is that it takes away from His actual authority as the God who came to correct His people. As a restorer, and in His authority, He explained the written Torah to those who would listen.

The Greatest Commandment

Thankfully, Yeshua offered us a summary of the Torah. Matthew 22:34–40 is one of my favorite passages in Scripture:

> *But the Pharisees, when they heard that Yeshua had silenced the Sadducees, gathered together in one place. And testing Him, one of them, a lawyer, asked, "Teacher, which is the greatest commandment in the Torah?"*
>
> *And He said to him, "'You shall love ADONAI your God with all your heart, and with all your soul, and with all your mind.' This is the first and greatest commandment. And the second is like it, 'You shall love your neighbor as yourself.' The entire Torah and the Prophets hang on these two commandments."*

Here is an example of this small group of outraged Pharisees asking Yeshua a fake question. They weren't interested in the answer; they just wanted to trap Him.

The first commandment Yeshua gave them was from the V'ahavta,[45] a prayer in Judaism that comes directly from Deuteronomy 6:5: "Love ADONAI your God with all your heart and with all your soul and with all your strength." This verse follows the Shema[46]—"Hear O Israel, the LORD our God, the LORD is one."—in Deuteronomy 6:4, which continues to be recited in synagogues every Shabbat. The V'ahavta is a prayer said in synagogues and in personal daily prayers. As with most Jewish prayers, it is named after the first few words of the prayer/verse itself. *V'ahavta* literally means, "And you shall love."

The second commandment was from Leviticus 19:18: "You are not to take vengeance, nor bear any grudge against the children of your people, but love your neighbor as yourself. I am

ADONAI." If you've never thought about keeping command-ments before and you're trying to figure these things out, Ye-shua says, "Hang all of it on these two things."

God commanded Jewish people to wear fringes (*tzitzit* in Hebrew) with blue in them to remind Jewish people to help us "look, remember, and observe" the commandments that God gave us through Moses.

> *ADONAI spoke to Moses saying, "Speak to Bnei-Yisrael. Say to them that they are to make for themselves tzitzit on the corners of their garments throughout their generations, and they are to put a blue cord on each tzitzit. It will be your own tzitzit—so whenever you **look** at them, you will **remember** all the mitzvot of ADONAI and do them and not go spying out after your own hearts and your own eyes, prostituting your-selves. This way you will remember and obey **(observe)** all My mitzvot and you will be holy to your God. I am ADONAI your God. I brought you out of the land of Egypt to be your God. I am ADONAI your God."*
>
> —***Numbers 15:37–41*** *(emphasis added)*

Traditionally, these fringes—with the strings, certain num-ber of knots, and the way they are tied—add up to 613, by some thought to be the amount of the commandments in the Torah. In verse 39 God told us that these fringes are for us to literally look at them. By looking at them, we will remember the com-mandments God gave us. When we remember the command-ments God gave us, we are then (verse 40) inspired to observe the commandments and be holy.

My professor in seminary, Dr. Bryan Widbin, a Hebrew scholar, told us that the word in Hebrew, *kadosh*, should not be translated as *holy* in English.[47] Rather, the word *kadosh* should be translated at "completely other." Why? Because God is completely other than His creation, and since humankind is made in His image, we are completely other than anything else in creation. Meaning, there is nothing like God in creation, and there is nothing in creation like people. By design, we are made to be completely other. When God made His covenant with the Jewish people, He said, "Be [completely other] as I am [completely other]" (Leviticus 19:2). This is the idea of separation. Israel, the Jewish people, are told to be separate from the nations, to be different, to be completely other than all the nations.

These fringes that we wear are a tangible reminder of our complete otherness. Traditionally, Orthodox Jews wear a *tallit katan*. The tallit katan is a fringed garment traditionally worn by Jewish males, either under or over one's clothing. It is a poncho-like garment with a hole for the head, with these special twined and knotted fringes known as *tzitzit* attached to its four corners. The idea of corners comes from verse 38: "...on the corners of their garments throughout their generations, and they are to put a blue cord on each tzitzit." These corners are also understood in Hebrew as the hem of this garment.[48]

From verse 38, God also commanded the tzitit would be blue. Why blue (or in some Jewish translations, violet)? Well, as in other traditions, blue/violet represents wealth.[49] So, this combination of fringes on corners of a garment and blue dye on a special hem, on this garment that represented one's authority, takes us to Jesus, who wore these same fringes: "And wherever He entered villages, towns, or countryside, people were placing the sick in the marketplaces and begging Him to let them touch even the tzitzit of His garment—and all who touched it were being healed" (Mark 6:56).

In Mark 5, we read about women with an issue of blood being "unclean":

> *Now if a woman has a discharge of her blood for many days not during her niddah or if she has a discharge beyond the time of her niddah all the days of the discharge of her uncleanness should be as in the days of her niddah. She is unclean. Every bed where she lies all the days of her discharge will be like her bed during her niddah, and everything she sits on will become unclean like the uncleanness of her niddah. Whoever touches these things will become unclean and is to wash his clothes and bathe himself in water, and be unclean until the evening.*
>
> —*Leviticus 15:25–27*

In every way, a woman with an issue of blood was unclean and literally untouchable—and sorry if you are reading this while eating, but women did not have tampons or pads in this time period (pun intended). Mark described the event when such a woman encountered Yeshua:

> *And there was a woman with a blood flow for twelve years, who had suffered much under many doctors. She had spent all that she had without benefit; instead, she grew worse. When she heard about Yeshua, she came through the crowd from behind and touched His garment. For she kept saying, "If I touch even His clothes, I shall be healed." Right away the blood flow stopped, and she felt in her body that she was healed from her disease. At once Yeshua, knowing in Himself that power had gone out from Him, turned around in the crowd and said, "Who touched My clothes?" His disciples responded, "You see the crowd pressing upon You and you say, 'Who touched Me?'" But He kept looking around to see who had done this.*
>
> *But the woman, scared and shaking, knowing what had happened to her, came and fell down before Him and told Him the whole truth. And He said to her, "Daughter, your faith*

has made you well. Go in shalom and be healed from your
disease."

—Mark 5:25–34

Why did she touch His garment (or as other translations note, "the hem of His garment")? Well, as noted above, His tzitzit hung from the corners of His garment, and the hem represented His authority, which came from His perfect keeping of the commandments, as His fringes represented. Go back to "look, remember, observe." Yeshua was sinless, meaning He didn't break any commandments. Which means He wore tzitzit and He looked, remembered, and observed perfectly.

Watch this: Yeshua was so pure and clean that when He touched someone unclean, they became clean. He could not be made unclean! But Leviticus says, "Whoever touches these things will become unclean" (Leviticus 15:27). That is, unless the one touching the unclean woman is so clean everything He touches becomes clean and He, being perfect and sinless, could not be made unclean by someone unclean.

This is how Yeshua tied it all together (again, pun intended) when He was asked what the greatest commandment was:

> *But the Pharisees, when they heard that Yeshua had silenced the Sadducees, gathered together in one place. And testing Him, one of them, a lawyer, asked, "Teacher, which is the greatest commandment in the Torah?"*
>
> *And He said to him, " 'You shall love ADONAI your God with all your heart, and with all your soul, and with all your mind.' This is the first and greatest commandment. And the second is like it, 'You shall love your neighbor as yourself.' The entire Torah and the Prophets hang on these two commandments."*
>
> *—Matthew 22:34–40*

Pump the brakes: "The entire Torah and the Prophets hang on these two commandments." Whoa! Does that mean you don't need commandments anymore? Was Jesus saying something new? No, He was simplifying what all the Pharisees around Him in this moment already know. If you love God and love your neighbor, you will keep all the commandments.

If you're keeping commandments out of guilt, shame, or fear of condemnation, then you shouldn't keep them, because that's not what they're for. They're not to make you feel bad about yourself. You keep commandments because you love God with all your heart, with all your soul, and with all your strength and you want to do what He asks you to do.

As a summary of a discussion in the Talmud regarding commandments in Makkot, the rabbis say that 613 commandments were given to Moses; King David reduced them to eleven (Psalm 15); Isaiah to six (Isaiah 33:15); Micah to three (Micah 6:8); Isaiah, a second time, to two (Isaiah 56:1); but Amos to one: "Seek Me and live!" (Amos 5:6, paraphrased). In the same way as the prophets who came before Him, Yeshua offered His version of a summary of all the commandments. "These two" are a summary, not a replacement, and certainly are not new, since both commandments He mentions are from the Torah. Summaries don't negate; they sum up.

Following God's commandments means you assume responsibility for the well-being of your neighbors. Everyone in this world can be considered your neighbor. Since you are responsible for your neighbors, some of the commandments have to do with loving people. But we will return to that in Chapter Three, "Justify Yourself." Let's get back to the fringes.

As noted, the tzitzit are usually attached to the four corners of a garment, but I attach them to two safety pins. I made the

decision that I would do this back when I was a teenager, because according to Yeshua, there are two commandments that
are the most important. For me, all the commandments literally
hang on "these two" safety pins. I've had other Jewish people
laugh at my explanation and tell me that I am wearing them
wrong, and they are right. I am not wearing them according to
normative tradition. Of course, they don't wear them right according to the text. Remember Numbers 15:38: "Speak to Bnei-
Yisrael. Say to them that they are to make for themselves tzitzit
on the corners of their garments throughout their generations,
and they are to put a blue cord on each tzitzit." Here is what
Chabad, an ultra-Orthodox Jewish organization, says about the
lack of blue in the fringes of most modern orthodox Jews:[50]

> The verse contains two requirements. One is to affix (white)
> fringes on the corners of a four-cornered garment, and the
> other is to add a thread of *tekhelet* to each corner. These two
> requirements are independent of each other. When *tekhelet*
> is available, we are enjoined to add a *tekhelet* fringe to the
> *tzitzit*; when unavailable, we fulfill the mitzvah with plain
> white fringes. The unique blue dye was made from a byprod-
> uct of a sea creature known as the *chilazon*, which lives in
> the Mediterranean Sea.
>
> So, why is it not so common today to have a *tekhelet* fringe
> on the *tallit* or *tzitzit*? At a certain point in history, approxi-
> mately 1000 years ago, the *chilazon*, which was always hard
> to come by—to the extent that the Talmud tells us that it sur-
> faced only once every seventy years—became unavailable
> altogether. After a while, its exact identity became unknown.
> There have been many who have tried to rediscover the iden-
> tity of the *chilazon*. Most notable among them were the
> Radziner rebbe, Rabbi Gershon Henoch Leiner (1839–
> 1891), and Israeli Chief Rabbi Y. I. Herzog (1888–1959).
> Rabbi Leiner maintained that the cuttlefish was the lost *chi-
> lazon*, and proceeded to produce and distribute dye produced
> from this fish. Recently, the marine snail *Murex trunculus*

has been identified as possibly being the elusive *chilazon*, and many use its dye.

The bottom line is that they follow the rabbis' opinions from the 1800s, and I follow my Rabbi, who is also God, who wrote the Torah. See, there is no requirement in the text of what exact blue, or what animal the dye comes from, or what region, or "if you can't find blue then don't wear it at all." So, because of what can only be called man-made rules, they negate the actual commandment that came from God. That is what made Yeshua most angry.

Yeshua did not command in the New Testament to wear the fringes on two safety pins. Safety pins weren't around yet. I am not claiming it is the right way to wear them. I am claiming that as a Jewish follower of Yeshua, I am obligated to wear fringes like my Messiah did, and as it is commanded for Jewish people in the book of Numbers. There are just more ways to do it than people want to admit or allow.

I am not saying to do whatever you want, either. This is the importance of being a part of community and under the authority of someone and something bigger than yourself. I wear my tzitzit the way I do because my dad wears them that way and we came up with a reason. Reasons for doing something become traditions. But for me, that is where it ends. It is a tradition, with good reason and logic, but wearing tzitzit on two safety pins is not a commandment from God. For Jewish people to wear them in the first place most certainly *is* a commandment.

According to the rabbis, I do not wear my tzitzit—the fringes described in Numbers 15:38–39—in the correct way. I usually wear them inside my pants, and they do properly represent the commandments. With the way they're tied, the strings and everything add up to 613.

Yeshua did not throw out any commandments, because He was not an innovator of something new when He came to earth as a baby and grew up as a Jewish man and rabbi in the land of Israel. No, He was more like a reformer or restorer.

The rabbis and Pharisees were not bad, wrong, or evil. They were human, and we all struggle with the same things. You just can't make a tradition a commandment and say it is from God if it is not actually from God.

The two greatest commandments are not an excuse not to keep the rest, even the one about not mixing different fabrics (Leviticus 19:19). You can get so concerned about trying to free yourself from the law that you forget that the main reason for keeping the law is your love of God and your love for your neighbor. Through His Holy Spirit, God gives you the ability to discern for yourself what you can and can't do and why you're doing these things in the first place. Sometimes He calls you to things, and sometimes He doesn't.

Commandments for Different Seasons

There are different commandments for Jews than there are for Gentiles, and there are different commandments for men and for women. There are different commandments for different seasons of your life, such as when you're a child, a parent, or a grandparent.

Confusion sets in when you mix and match commandments. Men cannot observe commandments for women (menstrual cycle). Woman cannot observe commandments for men (seminal emissions). Gentiles are not obligated to observe command-ments for Jews like circumcision, the sabbath, feasts, and not eating unclean food. We will deal with this more in depth later.

You must stop treating the commandments like they're black and white, like they're right and wrong things and you have to try to do all the right ones. That's not how it works. There are different moments, different seasons in your life when you're supposed to step back and ask God, "Am I doing what's right in this season?" Then, you need to listen to Him when He speaks.

If you are striving to keep the two greatest command-ments—to love the Lord your God with all your heart, all your soul, and all your strength, and to love your neighbor as your-self—you're going to do everything that you're supposed to be doing.

These things will not come to fruition today, tomorrow, or even in the next week. It's a lifetime of struggling with these things, paying attention to God, and reading His Word on your own. Don't just listen to people speak to you about the Bible. Read it. Wrestle with it. Struggle with it. Allow God to speak to you through His Holy Spirit.

Sermons confirm what God is already saying. He is speak-ing to you all the time; you must take the time to hear what He has to say. It's all there in Scripture.

Pay Attention to What God Is Saying

The more you read God's Word, and the more you pay at-tention to it, the more you will see Him use it in your life. The more you read through it and find different verses in different seasons of your life, the more you'll find yourself saying, "Oh, man! I never saw this before. It changes everything for me."

> *And He said to him, "'You shall love ADONAI your God with all your heart, and with all your soul, and with all your mind.' This is the first and greatest commandment. And the second is like it, 'You shall love your neighbor as yourself.' The entire Torah and the Prophets hang on these two commandments."*
>
> **—Matthew 22:37–40**

Jesus never said anything new. It was all found in the Hebrew Scriptures—the Torah, the Writings, the Prophets, and even in Jewish tradition. Judaism is not bad, and Christianity isn't better. We all have the same problems, because we're all human beings. We miss the point often, even when it's right in front of us and being explained very clearly, and we run after the things we shouldn't.

Just as in the day when He sent Yeshua, God continues to call us back to Himself. He is saying, "Stop striving for religion and just listen. Open your ears. Pay attention."

CHAPTER THREE

"But I Say..."

As we have previously established, Jesus taught ancient truth with authority. He is the Word of God in the flesh (John 1:14), and He is calling people to turn back to God—not just a few thousand years ago in the stories you read about Him, but today.

John 4 records Yeshua's famous conversation with the Samaritan woman at Jacob's well. Look at what she said to Him at the end of the conversation: "The woman tells Him, 'I know that Messiah is coming (He who is called the Anointed One.) When He comes, He will explain everything to us'" (John 4:25). There was an expectation in first-century Israel, and even in Judaism today, that when the Messiah shows up, He'll explain it all. It's not all going to sound totally brand new. In fact, it'll probably sound similar to the things that came before. He's just going to explain it for us in a way that it's never been explained before.

According to one Orthodox rabbi, there is an opinion that when the Messiah comes, the only books of the Bible that will be regularly studied are the five books of Moses. "The reason for this," he says, "is that all the other teachings of the prophets can be derived from the Torah, and since the Messiah will reveal all the meanings of the Torah to perfection, the prophetic writings will no longer be needed."[51]

Though I understand this rabbi's perspective, I don't necessarily agree with everything he says here. When Yeshua returns, I don't know that we'll really need any Scripture since He is God's Word in the flesh.

When Yeshua came the first time, however, He did exactly what this rabbi said He would do. He explained the Torah, and what He explained seriously upset some people because He equated Himself with God. He said He was God and that He could forgive people's sins. He messed with the establishment.

The Root of Sin

When I make the point that Jesus didn't say anything new, some people point out Matthew 5, where Jesus said, "You have heard that it was said … but I tell you…" (Matthew 5:21–48). That sounds like He was about to say something new and different from what the other rabbis of His day were saying, right? Yet that's not, in fact, the heart of what's happening in Matthew 5.

After making it clear that He did not come to abolish the Torah, but to fulfill it, Yeshua delivered a long teaching sermon to His audience, which included some Pharisees. He discussed murder, adultery, divorce, oaths, the concept of an eye for an eye and a tooth for a tooth, and how you should love your enemies.

Most people read these as Yeshua saying, "Look, you've

heard it taught this way, but what I say to you is totally different." What He was actually doing, however, was calling people back to the Scriptures.

We have a list of things about which we believe, so long as we haven't done them, we're still good people. Yeshua took that list and said, "No, no, no. It's much bigger than if you've ever murdered anyone. It's much bigger than if you've ever committed adultery. It's much harder than that to follow God."

Preaching and teaching often focuses on the fact that the best is yet to come—which is true—but sometimes you can take the encouragement of that message and twist it to avoid dealing with your sin. You're a good person. You love your spouse, your children, your family, and you've never killed anyone, so what does God have to do in you? But Yeshua said:

> *You have heard it was said to those of old, "You shall not murder, and whoever commits murder shall be subject to judgment." But I tell you that everyone who is angry with his brother shall be subject to judgment. And whoever says to his brother, "Raca"[52] shall be subject to the council; and whoever says, "You fool!" shall be subject to fiery Gehenna.[53]*
>
> **—Matthew 5:21–22**

Obviously, Yeshua was not giving you permission to murder. He was telling you to not even be angry in your heart. Why did He bring up anger in talking about murder? When He used the words "anger" and "murder," every one of His Jewish listeners would have thought of Cain and Abel, the perpetrator and the victim of the first murder in history. Genesis 4:3–7 sets the stage for us:

So it happened after some time that Cain brought an offering of the fruit of the ground to ADONAI, while Abel—he also brought of the firstborn of his flock and their fat portions. Now ADONAI looked favorably upon Abel and his offering, but upon Cain and his offering He did not look favorably. Cain became very angry, and his countenance fell.

Then ADONAI said to Cain, "Why are you angry? And why has your countenance fallen? If you do well, it will lift. But if you do not do well, sin is crouching at the doorway. Its desire is for you, but you must master it."

So, what did Cain do in verse 8? "Cain spoke to Abel his brother. While they were in the field, Cain rose up against Abel his brother and killed him."

Yeshua continued in the Gospel of Matthew:

Therefore if you are presenting your offering upon the altar, and there remember that your brother has something against you, leave your offering there before the altar and go. First be reconciled to your brother, and then come and present your offering.

—Matthew 5:23–24

Who presented an offering at the altar that wasn't accepted, and it made them angry? Cain. And he was so angry that he killed his brother. As Jedi Grand Master Yoda once said, "Fear is the path to the dark side. Fear leads to anger. Anger leads to hate. Hate leads to suffering."[54] This was really Yeshua's point: hate in your heart is the first step toward murder.

How many times have you hated someone in your heart? How many times have people made you so angry that you thought things would be better if they weren't here? Murder, whether it's premeditated or in the heat of the moment, always involves anger.

No one listening to Yeshua's teaching on this matter walked away thinking, "Man, the rabbis never said that. They told us not to murder, but now Yeshua is telling us to not even be angry." No, it's there in the book of Genesis, in the Torah. It's tied to offerings that you make while you're still angry. Yeshua was saying that it would be better if you didn't make that offering at all. Deal with your anger first, and then come back and make the offering. God doesn't want you to be like Cain. Sin was crouching at the doorway, waiting to destroy him, and sin is waiting to destroy you, too.

It's much bigger than whether you're a good person. It's much bigger than whether you've committed murder. It's harder than that, and it always has been harder than that to do the things God has called you to do. Doing what God is calling you to do in your life means that you have to deal with yourself. *True* You have to deal with your own sin, including some of the ways you think and some of the things you hope for and put your heart into that are taking the place of God.

You're not a good person just because you haven't murdered anyone. Even people who have murdered someone are not worse than you. We're all in the same place. We've all had anger in our hearts.

Lust

Yeshua continued:

> You have heard that it was said, "You shall not commit adultery." But I tell you that everyone who looks upon a woman to lust after her has already committed adultery with her in his heart. And if your right eye causes you to stumble, gouge

it out and throw it away! It is better for you that one part of your body should be destroyed, than that your whole body be thrown into Gehenna. And if your right hand causes you to stumble, cut it off and throw it away! It is better for you that one part of your body should be destroyed, than that your whole body go into Gehenna.

—Matthew 5:27–30

Maybe you haven't physically committed adultery, but when you look at a woman or a man with lust, you're committing adultery with them in your heart. Yeshua was saying that what's happening internally is more important than what's happening externally. Your words and your actions are just a small glimpse into what's going on in your heart. If you want to follow Yeshua, you need to work out the inside. He is calling you to something higher.

Those of you who have been believers in Yeshua for a long time have a tendency to show up to service nicely dressed and well-made-up and convey that everything is great in your life. Internally, however, you're dying, and you don't want to talk about it because it makes you uncomfortable. You don't want to address it, but Yeshua said that you must. Adultery is not the line; even looking with lust at another person is.

Please don't gouge out one of your eyes or cut off your hand and say, "Rabbi Matt told me to," because that's not what we're talking about in this text. Yeshua is telling you to deal with the issue instead of running away from it. So many people are running away from addictions to pornography or refusing to deal with issues with sex and sexuality because they're uncomfortable to talk about. I know it's not comfortable, but you still need to deal with these things. Sin is crouching at your doorway, waiting to destroy you, but you can master it because of the sacrifice that Yeshua made for you. You don't have to be won over by sin.

Divorce

Yeshua then addressed the topic of divorce:

> *It was said, "Whoever sends his wife away, let him give her a certificate of divorce." But I say to you that everyone who divorces his wife, except for sexual immorality, makes her commit adultery; and whoever marries a divorced woman commits adultery.*
>
> *—Matthew 5:31–32*

This is a hard word in a culture where divorce is considered acceptable. I'm not saying that there's never a reason for divorce. In fact, Yeshua gave a reason: unfaithfulness. He went into more detail on the matter in a conversation with the Pharisees:

> *They said to Him, "Why then did Moses command to 'give her a certificate of divorce and put her away?'" Yeshua said to them, "Because of your hardness of heart Moses permitted you to divorce your wives, but from the beginning it was not so."*
>
> *—Matthew 19:7–8*

As the One who was there from the beginning, Yeshua was saying that the only reason that command was in the Torah in the first place was because they knew it would be needed, not because it was okay to divorce your wife. The issue at hand here is not divorce; it's your own heart.

In Second Temple Jewish culture, and even in Orthodox Judaism today, a man could divorce his wife because of the commandment in which Moses said they could give their wife a certificate of divorce (Deuteronomy 24:1–5). Men divorced their wives for the smallest reasons. If they don't like her anymore, or if they no longer find her attractive, they can divorce her. I'd suggest they take a good look in the mirror, because as we've gotten older, my wife has become even more beautiful, and she's definitely more attractive than I am.

Don't use the Torah to justify bad decisions. Don't use the Torah to lead yourself and other people into sin. And yet, some do this all the time. You may justify your actions by one verse, and ignore the verses that condemn you.

Yeshua was not condemning the Pharisees' teachings, but He was condemning their actions, for just like other leaders in other times and places, some of them were doing the wrong things and had no heart toward repentance. He was calling Israel back to Him, just as God is calling you back to Himself.

Revenge

Yeshua then moved on to the topic of revenge:

> *You have heard that it was said, "An eye for an eye, and a tooth for a tooth." But I tell you, do not resist an evildoer. But whoever slaps you on your right cheek, turn to him also the other. And the one wanting to sue you and to take your shirt, let him also have your coat. Whoever forces you to go one mile, go with him two. Give to the one who asks of you, and do not turn away from the one who wants to borrow from you.*
>
> *—Matthew 5:38–42*

Interestingly, when you look up the scriptures that reference this commandment in the Torah, it's only to be applied in very specific situations. In fact, one of the situations is so specific—if two men are fighting and hit a pregnant woman and she miscarries, or the baby is born with injuries as a result (Exodus 21:22–25)—it's hard to imagine it happening in the first place. However, the people were taking this commandment of an eye for an eye and a tooth for a tooth and applying it to every situation. We still do this today, insisting that regardless of the situation, we're owed what was taken away from us.

In the Roman culture Jesus was speaking into, Roman soldiers could force people to carry their gear while they ran a mile and make them go another mile ahead. Yeshua was reminding the people that the commandment of an eye for an eye and a tooth for a tooth did not apply to every situation. Scripture also tells us that vengeance belongs to the Lord (Deuteronomy 32:35).

Sometimes you have to take a step back and ask yourself and the Lord: Am I reacting to a person or a situation because I want vengeance and I want to get what belongs to me, or can I be content with the undeserved grace that God has given me, to the point that I can just give it all away? Can I trust that vengeance is the Lord's instead of taking matters into my own hands?

What Yeshua was talking about in this lengthy teaching sermon in Matthew 5 is the misapplication of the Scriptures. People who don't believe in the Bible will say people have used the Bible to justify all kinds of evil—slavery, a patriarchal society, the mistreatment of women. And that's true. But that's not the Bible's fault. That's the fault of people.

People have always been the problem. As long as you're a

human being, you're going to be a problem for yourself and what you actually want to believe. You can use the Bible to justify everything that you do so that you can commit more sin instead of reading the Bible to learn how to be more like God. Yeshua doesn't want you to apply Scripture incorrectly just because others have done it that way. He wants you to apply Scripture the way He meant it when He wrote it.

Loving Your Neighbor

Lastly, Yeshua addressed the issue of loving your neighbor:

> *You have heard that it was said, "You shall love your neighbor and hate your enemy." But I tell you, love your enemies and pray for those who persecute you, so that you may be children of your Father in heaven. He causes His sun to rise on the evil and the good, and sends rain on the righteous and the unrighteous. For if you love those who love you, what reward do you have? Even the tax collectors do the same, don't they? And if you greet only your brothers, what more are you doing than anyone else? Even the pagans do that, don't they? Therefore be perfect, just as your Father in heaven is perfect.*
> *—Matthew 5:43–48*

This passage is interesting because while the Scriptures certainly tell you to love your neighbor, nowhere does it tell you to hate your enemies. This part about hating your enemies seems to be something that was commonly said at the time.

Yeshua made it clear that loving the people you know is easy. That's not what you're called to, as followers of God. You're called to love even your enemies and to pray that God would turn them around.

My dad likes to tell a story about my brother Jake, who is

now a rabbi in Chicago. When he was about eight years old, he asked my dad, "Why don't we just pray for the salvation of the devil? If we could get him saved, everything would stop." This is why Jake has a doctorate in theology, because even as a child, he was asking questions that no one else asked.

My dad replied, "Well, son, the devil has gone too far, and he's too far gone. There's no praying for him, but there's no person in this world that's too far gone for God to reach where they are."

Even the worst people who do the worst things should be prayed for, because it's easy to love your neighbor but it's a whole other thing to love your enemy. The more you love on your enemies, the more you see yourself in them, because all these things come back to dealing with yourself.

Go Deeper with God

Don't use the Scriptures to justify your sin. Don't get stuck in saying, "I'm a good person. I've never murdered anybody, I've never committed adultery, I pray for my enemies, and I do all those things." Sometimes you use that language to make it seem like you're done—like God has completed His work in you and you have already been perfected.

God, however, wants to go deeper with you than that one thing you probably didn't do. Look at all the things you are do-ing and the decisions you're making, and the blessings you're missing out on, because you feel like you're all set and God doesn't need to do anything else in you. People who follow God sometimes stop short and refuse to go deeper with Him because we're afraid of how He's going to respond to us. The truth is, He knows all the thoughts you've ever had. Nothing is hidden from Him. You don't confess your sins to God to let Him know about them—He already knows! Confession and repentance are for you so that your sins don't stay hidden and keep you from running away from what He actually wants to do with your life.

The greater application is that some of the distractions you're facing are happening right now. You might be thinking, "That's not true. I'm just too busy. For me, it's something else happening." But that's simply not the case. The issue is inside of you, in your heart and in your mind. God can change your entire life if you just give everything to Him and repent of your sins.

Maybe you haven't committed "big" sins like murder or adultery, or maybe you have. Either way, we're all sinners. There is sin in our lives, and the sin is evident to you in the thoughts you have throughout the course of your day. You already know them, because when you have those thoughts, you often stop yourself and go, "I don't even know where that came from." That's the stuff God wants to deal with, in your heart and in your mind, so that you can be a more fully devoted follower of Yeshua.

It's not about pointing the finger at other people's sin, and it's not about the people who have misused the Scriptures and misrepresented God. All of that is real and true, but they can become excuses for not dealing with yourself. You need to stop and allow God to speak to you. He's constantly saying, "You've heard it said this way, but if you'd just listen to Me for a minute, it would change everything."

It's Time to Deal with It

Maybe you're reading this and thinking, "I didn't really like that." Later today, when you're dealing with what you didn't really like, ask the Lord, "What do I need to deal with? What do You want to change in me? I'm done with all the voices that are speaking all the things they're speaking. I want to hear You more clearly. Would You please open my ears and help me to listen for what You're actually saying so that I can make some real changes in my life?"

I know God loves those prayers more than any other—those prayers when you come to the end of yourself and say, "I need You. I'm not even sure how I need You. I just know I can't do this by myself."

Would you commit to praying that today? Regardless of what distractions are going on in your life, would you commit to asking the Lord, "What do I need to change? What do You have that's better for me, that I'm missing? What's the real heart of the matter that I'm not paying attention to?"

Anger
Resentment
Feeling of injustice
Can't deal c this on my own

CHAPTER FOUR

Justify Yourself

Yeshua, as we've discussed previously, was not an innovator. He was a restorer. His goal was to repair first-century Judaism and return it to its original, intended condition. Most of the arguments He had with the Pharisees, Sadducees, and Essenes were not about content. They were about who He is as both man and God—as the Messiah.

In the Talmud, the Mishnah, and the various writings of the first-century rabbis, you will find very similar things to what Yeshua said. For example, Rabbi Hillel, one of the most important rabbis in first-century Judaism, said something very similar to "Love your neighbor as yourself."[55] Why? Because they're all quoting the Torah. These weren't ideas that they came up with themselves. They weren't philosophers in the sense of Socrates and Plato, who thought of and said things no one had ever said before. No, they were speaking from the Hebrew Scriptures.

The other first-century rabbis didn't understand that Yeshua was the Word in the flesh (John 1:14). He would never go against Scripture, because the words that make up Scripture make Him up as a person. There's therefore nothing new in what He says. Yeshua speaks with authority; He doesn't speak opinions. As people, we interpret Scripture from the way we read it. We pick what works for us. Yeshua, on the other hand, explained what He meant when He wrote it. Expressing the commands differently, and making them more difficult to follow, doesn't make them new.

Adding More Rules

The difficulty is, when the rabbis talk about "commandments," they not only meant the commandments found in the Torah, but also various other man-made commandments they added. This happened as they tried to flesh out how commandments worked in everyday life. Many of these additional "commandments" are the radical innovations that Yeshua argued against.

Remember, "Jesus' Judaism was a conservative reaction against some radical innovations in the Law stemming from the Pharisees and Scribes of Jerusalem."[56] Yeshua was not against tradition or keeping traditions. He was always against treating traditions as commandments and telling people they must keep traditions like commandments.

The New Testament is not a dramatic shift from the Scriptures that came before it. The New Testament is just as Jewish as the rest of the Hebrew Scriptures. It cannot be that we have the Hebrew Scriptures and the Christian New Testament, since almost all of the New Testament was written by Jewish people.[57] The apostles, including Paul (who often is blamed as the one who left Judaism), never stop adhering to Judaism, but they did reexamine some conclusions about the Scriptures and the way they understood them prior to Yeshua.

Frustratingly, Andy Stanley writes this about Paul:

> Paul immediately saw the problems associated with blending the old with the new. As an educated Pharisee who spent his adult life studying, teaching, and defending the law, he instantly recognized the incompatibility of Moses and Jesus. From day one, he recognized Jesus was not an add-on or a continuation of the old ways. In Jesus, he recognized the introduction of something brand-new. The new he recognized encompassed more than who was included in the kingdom of God and who wasn't....prior to his conversion, Paul recognized the incongruence of Moses and Jesus. The two were incompatible and unbendable. He didn't view the Jesus movement as a new version of Judaism. He viewed it as a perversion that must be eradicated.[58]

The incongruence is not with Moses and Jesus—Moses and Jesus agreed—but rather some of the Pharisaical additions to the Torah that were incompatible with both Moses and Jesus. Jesus' Judaism was real Judaism, but the Judaism that won out historically was the Judaism of the Pharisees, as they took authority after the destruction of the Temple and continued in some of the things Yeshua warned them against in the Gospels. This is why I say often that Messianic Judaism is not Judaism plus Jesus, or Jesus plus Judaism. Rather, Messianic Judaism is the Judaism of Jesus.

Stanley also writes, "The law was good, but the law was temporary. The law, and everything associated with it, was a means to an end. And the end had come. The law had a purpose. So mixing, matching, blending, cherry-picking, and retrofitting were not options for Paul. He insisted they weren't options for any Jesus follower."[59]

Paul never insisted that fellow Jews should stop being Jewish or practicing Judaism and then become Gentile Christians in practice. Paul, along with all of the Jewish apostles, insisted that in light of Yeshua, some of what they understood was not true and had to be adjusted or fixed. It's not mixing and matching what some call "Old" and "New" covenants. It is the mixing of things commanded by God with things "commanded" by men. N.T. Wright, in his fantastic work *Paul: A Biography,* said:

> Paul's experience in meeting Yeshua on the road to Damascus shattered Saul's wildest dreams and, at the same split second, fulfilled them. This was—he saw it in that instant—the fulfillment of Israel's ancient scriptures, but also the utter denial of the way he had been reading them up to that point.[60]

The utter denial of the Torah or Judaism? No, the utter denial of "the way he had been reading them." He kept reading, living, and following, but much of what he understood shifted in light of who Yeshua was. Paul, like Yeshua and all of His original, Jewish followers, never told Jewish people to stop keeping commandments. Rather, they encouraged both Jews and Gentiles to stick to the actual commandments found in the Torah and not concern ourselves with treating traditions that we create as if they were given to us by God.

Wright continues:

> What drove Paul, from the moment on the Damascus Road and throughout his subsequent life, was the belief that Israel's God had done what he had always said he would; that Israel's scriptures had been fulfilled in ways never before imagined; and that Temple and Torah themselves were not after all the ultimate realities, but instead glorious signposts

pointing forward to the new heaven-and-earth reality that had come to birth in Jesus. Paul remained to his dying day fiercely loyal to Israel's God, seen in a fresh and blinding focus in Jesus.[61]

In fact, there is no evidence that Paul stopped being a Pharisee. So many of the beliefs that the Pharisees taught found their way into Paul's letters, like the resurrection of Israel, belief in angels and demons, circumcision for Jews, immersion in water, and more. His zeal for the God of Israel never changed.

Yeshua was not against the Pharisees, either! He lovingly, and often angrily (like other prophets before Him), called them away from their radical innovations and back to Himself, as God. Their radical innovations are what is known as the "Traditions of the Elders," or the oral Torah. Separate but connected to the written Torah (five books of Moses) is the fleshing out of all the things the written word doesn't cover. This fleshing out is called "oral Torah" because it was transmitted through stories, disagreements, and arguments that were later compiled as the Talmud, a few hundred years after Yeshua.

Understand, tradition is not bad. The fleshing out of traditions is not bad. But when a tradition is treated as "God commands us to do this," when He actually didn't, well, that is what made Yeshua so angry. And I would argue, like Andy Stanley, that we ought not to teach tradition as being from God. This is the mixing and matching that is truly so dangerous—mixing actual written commandments that God gave to Moses with later, added traditions that we teach as if they were commanded by God when they are not.

The Good Samaritan

Most people, regardless of how familiar they are with the Bible, know the Parable of the Good Samaritan. Here's the premise I'm going to give you up front: the Parable of the Good Samaritan is not Jesus illuminating the vastness of who your neighbor is. It has to do with asking insincere questions.

In Luke 10, a Torah scholar asked Jesus, "Who is my neighbor?" Jesus responded by telling the Parable of the Good Samaritan. Remember how we talked about asking fake questions, in Chapter One? Such questions are asked not because the person asking sincerely desires an answer but because they're trying to trip up the other person.

> Now a certain Torah lawyer stood up to entrap Yeshua, saying, "Teacher, what should I do to gain eternal life?" Then Yeshua said to him, "What has been written in the Torah? How do you read it?" And he replied, "You shall love ADONAI your God with all your heart, and with all your soul, and with all your strength, and with all your mind; and your neighbor as yourself." Yeshua said to him, "You have answered correctly. Do this and you will live." But wanting to vindicate himself, he said to Yeshua, "Then who is my neighbor?"
>
> —*Luke 10:25–29*

Any Torah scholar or rabbi knows that the answer to "Who is my neighbor?" is "everyone." Yeshua was dealing with a fake question, an insincere question that hoped for a different answer than the one it already had. And it's not just the Pharisees and the Torah scholars who have done this. We, too, are often insincere in asking questions.

Yeshua responded to this question with a parable, which is a common method of explaining things in Judaism:

> Yeshua replied, "A certain man was going down from Jerusalem to Jericho. He was attacked by robbers, who stripped him and beat him. Then they left, abandoning him as half dead. And by chance, a kohen[62] was going down that road; but when he saw the man, he passed by on the opposite side. Likewise a Levite also, when he came to the place and saw him, passed by on the opposite side. But a Samaritan who was traveling came upon him; and when he noticed the man, he felt compassion. He went up to him and bandaged his wounds, pouring on olive oil and wine. Then setting him on his own animal, he brought him to a lodge for travelers and took care of him. The next day he took out two denarii and gave them to the innkeeper, saying, 'Take care of him. And whatever else you spend, upon my return I will repay you myself.' Which of these three seems to you a neighbor to the one attacked by robbers?" And he said, "The one who showed mercy to him." Then Yeshua said to him, "Go, and you do the same."
>
> —*Luke 10:30–37*

Yeshua never answered the question, "Who is my neighbor?" The answer given was: "The one who showed mercy to him. ... Go, and you do the same."

I'd like to draw your attention to a few phrases in these passages. First, verse 25 says that the Torah scholar was looking to entrap Yeshua. If you're asking a question to entrap somebody, is that a real question? Deuteronomy 18 encourages you to test those who speak in God's name. It's okay to ask questions, but entrapment goes beyond that. When you're trying to entrap someone with a question, you're hoping they're going to give the wrong answer.

My favorite entrapment question is when people ask me if I

believe in tithing. When I respond that I do, they then explain to me why they don't. They didn't care what my answer was; they just wanted to show me why they think I'm wrong.

You've experienced it, and, to be honest, we've all done it. You're not looking for an answer, and you're not even interested in the opinion of the person you're asking the question. You just want them to say the wrong thing so that you can pounce on them and say, "Ha! Well, that's not what I believe!"

When the Torah scholar asked Yeshua what he should do to gain eternal life, Yeshua did a very Jewish thing, which was to answer a question with a question: "What's been written in the Torah? How do you read it?"

The Torah scholar answered his own question, citing the two greatest commandments: to love God and to love your neighbor. These have always been considered the two greatest commandments in Judaism, by the way—Yeshua was not new in singling them out. Yeshua told the Torah scholar that he had answered correctly: if he did these things, he would live. They believed the same thing. Conversation over, right?

Nope. Verse 29 says that the Torah scholar wanted to "vindicate himself." Some translations say he wanted to "justify himself" (CJB). He followed up by asking Yeshua, "Then who is my neighbor?"

Yeshua wasn't just fully God—He was fully man, also. Accordingly, I have to believe that in this situation, He wanted to respond in a way similar to what you or I would say: "You're a Torah scholar and you don't know who your neighbor is? Really?"

As we've discussed previously, the Pharisees were not evil, and it's important we understand that. In fact, they were doing

their job by testing Yeshua, because that's what the Torah commanded them to do. If someone claims to be the Messiah, you
have to test him and ask him questions. You need to make sure
he's speaking from the Scriptures about the things of God and
that the things he promises actually take place. There's nothing
wrong with the Torah scholar's original question about how to
gain eternal life. It's a legitimate question to ask of the Messiah.
Yeshua answered His question, and they agreed.

But then the Torah scholar wanted to justify himself. I can't
tell you how often this happens to me, and to other rabbis and
pastors. When people find out I'm a rabbi, they feel a need to
prove to me their knowledge of the Scriptures. And that's exactly what happened with this Torah scholar and Yeshua.

Every time Jesus was entrapped, He turned it around and
entrapped the person who was trying to entrap Him. This is
what made Him so amazing in these moments. Jesus responded
by telling a parable about a priest and a Levite who ignore an
injured man by the side of the road. The Torah scholar who
asked the question may have been a priest or a Levite, and there
were likely priests and Levites in the audience listening to Him.

The hero of the story, the one who helped the injured man,
was a Samaritan. The Samaritans were half-Jewish and half-
Syrian, and were looked down upon by the Jewish people. They
created their own religion, worshiping on Mount Gerizim instead of at the Temple.[63] Yeshua took the one person who, from
the perspective of His listeners, shouldn't understand how to
love their neighbor, and made them the example.

The Torah scholar thought he was so wise and had asked
such a great question, but Yeshua flipped it around and made
him say, in front of the priests and the Levites, that the Samar-

itan was the neighbor in the story. It's no wonder that his conversation with Yeshua ended there: he was probably so embarrassed by what had happened that there was no other option than to walk away.

Asking the Right Questions, the Right Way

Yeshua spoke with such clarity and authority that every time He was entrapped, the person who tried to entrap Him ended up looking like a fool at the end of the conversation. The question, "Who is my neighbor?" was an insincere question, and insincerity subverts justice. It makes us miss the whole point.

We pride ourselves on being sincere, and yet, much of what we do and say is very insincere. The only possible outcome of this is the insincere person looking like a fool. There's an honesty in communication that needs to happen internally before you can communicate with sincerity externally, and most people who are insincere are insincere because they don't like what's happening on the inside. Such people are not trying to be dishonest or deceitful. In fact, most of them have no idea they're being insincere.

You are called to be honest with yourself first, then honest with God and others. You are supposed to ask questions to help you follow God better, not to try to trick, trap, or make a point. So, you need to think about the questions you ask before you ask them and the words you speak before you speak them. This doesn't just affect your external life. It affects your prayer life as well, because you may also be insincere in your requests to God—meaning, you want what you want regardless of God's stance.

When you ask God for something and He doesn't give it to

you because He wants to do something else, how do you respond? You may continue to pursue what you asked for, because you weren't really interested in God's answer. Anyone who has young children in their lives knows what this is like. The child is so desperately convinced that they need something and that you can fulfill that need, but you know they don't really need that toy or that piece of candy. Even so, it's next to impossible to convince them of that truth.

Rabbi Abraham Joshua Heschel once said, "We are closer to God when we are asking questions than when we think we have the answers."[64] You're supposed to ask questions. Asking questions is not the problem. What you need to understand is why you're asking a question and whether you really want an answer to it. Are you looking for people to agree with you—and if not, you walk away—or are you truly willing to hear the answer?

One thing that frustrates people about Judaism is that there aren't a whole lot of answers. What Judaism does extremely well is push people to ask the right questions, and the right questions don't have answers you are privy to. But asking the right questions with sincerity and the right intent can change your life.

Too often, you can be like that Torah scholar, getting stuck in the insincerity of your question because you're trying to justify or vindicate yourself. You're trying to prove yourself to God or to people. You don't want to say, "I don't know," because people will walk away thinking, "Well, he doesn't know, and he's supposed to know." But sometimes, you just don't know!

There's an insincerity in your question-asking and in your response. Sigmund Freud once said, "Where the questions of religion are concerned people are guilty of every possible sort of dishonesty and intellectual misdemeanor." [65] It's so true. We say things to people like, "You're just going to have to figure it out for yourself," or, "Maybe you don't have enough faith."

When it comes to religion, sometimes you might overlook the fact that we all are human. You look at people who are struggling with things that you have overcome, and you wonder why they can't overcome them the way you did. You forget that people have their own journeys and their own stories. Instead, you can get wrapped up in religiosity—what you're supposed to do and what everyone else is supposed to be doing. You love to tell others what they should be doing, but there's an insincerity that's happening in your own heart.

George Orwell explains this quite nicely: "The great enemy of clear language is insincerity. When there is a gap between one's real and one's declared aims, one turns, as it were, instinctively to long words and exhausted idioms, like a cuttlefish squirting out ink."[66]

There was a gap between the declared aim of the Torah scholar and his intended aim. He declared that he wanted to know who his neighbor was, but his intent was to vindicate himself. And Yeshua looked right into his heart and said, "If the one who's the neighbor in this story is the one who gives mercy, then maybe you should start there."

So often, you too can try to vindicate yourself, to justify your words and your actions through religion and spirituality. You try to justify the things you do, the things you don't do, and the things everyone else is supposed to do, because you think you figured it all out a long time ago.

This is some hard stuff to process. It's real, and it's honest. I became a rabbi because I love questions. My father, who is a

Messianic rabbi in New York, encouraged my brothers and me to ask questions from the time we were young, and no question was ever off the table. Dad never dismissed us because of our age, especially when it came to questions about the Scriptures.

One of these moments occurred at the Bible study my father taught every Tuesday night. I was fifteen years old at the time, and a man who was not a believer in Yeshua approached my dad at the end of the study. Of course, he hadn't listened to anything my dad taught during the study, because he had an insincere question on his mind. He was just there to play Stump the Rabbi.

I was standing next to my dad when the man asked him this question: "My grandfather was an observant Jew who never heard the gospel. He died having never heard about Jesus. Is he in heaven, or is he in hell?"

My dad replied, "I'm not the judge of where people go, and I don't know where your grandfather is. But you just heard the gospel tonight, and I can tell you where you're going if you reject Yeshua."

I was amazed. My dad took that man's question and flipped it on him, Yeshua-style. Rabbis, myself included, get questions like that all the time. Some make the mistake of trying to answer theologically, but my dad cut to the heart of it. He knew the man wasn't really concerned about his grandfather's salvation; he was worried about his own. And my dad gave it to him straight.

George W. Bush made an amazing statement that should be framed and hung on the wall in every home, business, and public place: "Too often, we judge other groups by their worst examples, while judging ourselves by our best intentions. ... And this has strained our bonds of understanding and common purpose."[67] You can be so busy pointing your finger at other people and talking about how awful they are that you forget you're just like them. Even if you've been walking with the Lord your entire life, there is still sin in you. Yet somehow, you're able to judge yourself according to your best intentions. You don't necessarily intend to—you know when you're wrong, and you tell yourself you won't do it again. Everyone else, however, you judge according to their worst examples.

Dealing with Your Insincerity

Yeshua did not tell the Parable of the Good Samaritan because He was trying to explain who your neighbor is. Because of the Torah, you already know that everyone is your neighbor. What it boiled down to was that sometimes when you are in a place of being insincere, you don't even realize you're being insincere. This subverts the justice that's supposed to be happening around you. It stops you from doing what God is asking you to do.

As an example, when you're out driving or walking and you encounter a homeless man with a sign asking for money, you tend to think, "I could give him money, but he'll probably spend it on drugs or alcohol, so I'm not going to do it." There may be a moment in between seeing the man and making your decision when you sense God asking you to help him, but you quickly talk yourself out of it and justify your decision based on what the man may or may not do with the money.

Next time, if you sense that God is asking you to give him money, just do it. You may not agree with this, and I can understand why you might not. But I recently saw such a man standing outside the 7-Eleven, and I asked him what he wanted. He answered honestly, "A pack of cigarettes and a beer," so I went in and bought them for him.

When I gave him the cigarettes and the beer, I told him I was a rabbi and said, "I'd love to talk to you more about these things, because I think we can get you some help so that you don't have to depend on them. But if this is where you're at, that's okay."

I want to encourage you to ask this question of the Lord: "Are the questions I ask You insincere, or am I using the questions I ask You to avoid asking the questions that would actually change my life?" Take the time to let Him respond to you.

You need to be in community so that you can bring your feelings, your fears, and the things you have heard and sort them out with the help of other believers. There is no place in the Scriptures where it says, "And you alone will speak to the Lord and only you, for you do not need anyone else to speak into your life."

But because we all wear so many masks all the time, we're afraid to open ourselves and discover who we really are. So, we're afraid to let other people in. You might say things like, "I just haven't found a place where I feel fed," or "I haven't found anywhere I really connect." There's no better place to find those things than in a community of believers who are all trying to be more sincere. Accept that you are an insincere person attempting to become more sincere because of the death and resurrection of your Messiah, Yeshua.

Examine yourself, and allow God to speak to you and actually help you. No matter how old you are or how long you've been walking with the Lord, He wants to help you be more sincere in your relationship with Him and communicate sincerely with the people around you. You may be so bound up on the inside that you don't even realize you're insincere. I believe that you can be set free from your insincerity, but the first step is being honest and acknowledging that as a fallen human being, insincerity is your default. Only through the power of Yeshua can you become more sincere as you open yourself up to God, to community, and to people who want to love you and have a relationship but can't—because they can't break through the barrier of insincerity.

The more you can break through these things in community, the healthier you will become. God will definitely work through a group that is filled with people who acknowledge that they're insincere but are working to become more sincere through the power of the Holy Spirit.

CHAPTER FIVE

Stop Sinning

Religion is not a bad thing, but people who consider themselves religious can take things too far. In Judaism, being religious is a positive thing. In Christianity, it's considered a negative thing. It's an interesting—and telling—difference.

This dichotomy matters because context and emphasis matter. For Jews, like myself but also including the most (non-messianic) orthodox in practice, being religious is good. We don't obey to be blessed; we obey to be a blessing. We don't obey to be protected; we obey to protect. Pagans believed that you don't make the gods angry (or else). That is the way that false gods demand worship and is the way that Greek mythology worked. But Jewish thought works differently, and being religious for a Jewish person is good because it brings us back to "look, remember, observe." Why? Because we were slaves in Egypt and God set us free! And we want everyone to experience freedom.

For many Christians, being religious is equated with harsh rule-following. In Judaism, the first step in commandment-keeping is recognizing you're not very good at keeping commandments—you are a sinner. So, stop sinning.

Whether you consider being religious a positive thing or a negative thing, you're likely wondering what you should do with your life and how you can live out your faith. Remember these two words: stop sinning. It's very important for your future and the future of everyone around you that you stop sinning.

In *The 613 Mitzvot* by Ronald L. Eisenberg, he discusses the organization of commandments by Maimonides: positive commandments in ten groups and negative commandments in ten groups.[68] Then Eisenberg notes what he calls "Rabbinic commandments," which are listed by Rambam as part of the 613. He describes "the Rabbi's established seven mitzvot that were not based on verse in the Torah." Included in these seven "commandments" are the washing of hands (we will come back later) and limitations in the movement and transfer of objects on Shabbat, both of which Yeshua deals with directly in the Gospels.

Let's deal with the latter first. Did Yeshua break the Sabbath? The story is in the Gospel of John:

After this there was a Jewish feast, and Yeshua went up to Jerusalem. Now in Jerusalem there is a pool by the sheep gate, called [Bethesda], which has five porches. In these a crowd of invalids was lying around—blind, lame, disabled. Now a certain man had been an invalid there for thirty-eight years. Seeing him lying there and knowing he had been that way a long time, Yeshua said to him, "Do you want to get well?" The invalid answered Him, "Sir, I have nobody to put me into the pool when the water is stirred up. While I'm trying to get in, somebody else steps down before me!" Yeshua tells him, "Get up! Pick up your mat and walk!" Immediately, the man was healed! He took up his mat and started walking around. Now that day was Shabbat, so Judean leaders were saying to the man who was healed, "It's Shabbat! It's not permitted for you to carry your mat." But he answered them, "The man who made me well told me, 'Pick up your mat and walk.'" They asked him, "Who is the man who told you, 'Pick up your mat and walk'?" But the man who had been healed didn't know who it was, for Yeshua had slipped away into the crowd in that place. Afterwards, Yeshua finds him in the Temple. He said to him, "Look, you've been healed! Stop sinning, so nothing worse happens to you." The man left and told the Judean leaders that it was Yeshua who had made him well. Because Yeshua was doing these things on Shabbat, the Judean leaders started persecuting Him. But Yeshua said to them, "My Father is still working, and I also am working." So for this reason the Judean leaders kept trying even harder to kill Him—because He was not only breaking Shabbat, but also calling God His own Father, making Himself equal with God.

—John 5:1–18

This is a fantastic story, but to better understand it, we need to start with the end rather than the beginning. Two accusations were made against Yeshua in verse 18, the last sentence of the passage. In some translations, it simply says "the Jews" (NASB) instead of "the Judean leaders," which has contributed in part to antisemitism. It wasn't all of the Jewish people; it wasn't even all of their leaders. It was the leaders who were there with Yeshua at that time.

As we've discussed previously, the Pharisees as a whole were not actually evil. They were just people, and today, we do the very same things they did. We love to make rules for ourselves and then make sure that everyone else keeps those rules, even if we can't. We like to judge people by these rules, which most of the time are not even found in Scripture.

Yeshua Never Broke the Sabbath

The first accusation these Jewish leaders made against Yeshua was that He broke the rules for the Sabbath. The second was that He was making Himself equal with God, which was true. He was calling Himself God. What these leaders misunderstood, however, was that Yeshua was not breaking the Sabbath.

If Yeshua broke the Sabbath, that means He broke a commandment from God, which means He sinned. If He sinned, He was not a kosher[69] sacrifice for the people because the sacrifice had to be without blemish and without sin. That's simply not possible, because Scripture tells us that Yeshua is the Passover lamb and that He offered Himself as a sacrifice for our sins (1 Corinthians 5:7).

What Yeshua broke were the extra rules for the Sabbath, the rules that were added by people after God commanded us to rest from our regular work on the Sabbath (Exodus 20:8–11). If you don't have the context of who Yeshua is as a Jewish person, it's easy to misunderstand the accusation of the Jewish leaders that Yeshua was breaking the Sabbath. He did not actually break the Sabbath, but that was how they interpreted His actions.

The Jewish leaders didn't like the fact that He had told this man to carry his mat on the Sabbath. From their perspective, it was against the rules that had been added to the observance of the Sabbath. Yeshua had no problem breaking man's added rules, but He never broke God's commandments.

So often, you build little walls of rules around yourself, telling yourself that as long as you don't break these rules, you'll be okay. They give you a false sense of security and safety—and even superiority. Eventually, you start to judge everyone else by these rules you've made up.

Here's an example of such a rule. Remember when our parents used to tell us not to sit too close to the TV because it would ruin our eyesight and we'd go blind? As we got older, we found out that wasn't really true. It might strain our eyes a little bit, but it wouldn't cause us to go blind.

On the spiritual level, such rules give you a false sense of holiness, leading you to believe that doing or not doing these things keeps you in right relationship with God. In reality, some of the most religious things about you may be killing you on the inside and cutting off your relationship with the Lord.

That's why Yeshua would get so angry in these conversations with the Pharisees. You also might elevate the rules you've made up above the commandments God has actually given you, and then blame it on Him, claiming that His commandments weren't any good to begin with or that you no longer need to obey them. The rules you make up for yourself prevent you from keeping God's commandments.

Come As You Are

In verse 14 of our passage from John 5, Yeshua told the man He just healed to stop sinning. He was speaking out of the heart of the Torah and the heart of God the Father as to how He wants His people to act. To paraphrase a quote from Andy Stanley, heartless people will say, "Change and you can join us." Yeshua says, "Join us and you will change."[70] Hypocrites want people to change before they're willing to have a relationship with them, but Yeshua invites us into a relationship with Him and promises us that this relationship will change us.

I have a great deal of respect for Lecrae and his music. He's a rapper who is also a Christian. He doesn't consider himself a "Christian rapper"—he often raps about God and about the Scriptures, but he raps about other things, too. Lecrae also collaborates with secular artists, people who are not religious by any definition of the word. Because of this, a lot of Bible-believing people attack Lecrae on social media, slandering him and questioning his character and his faith. And yet, Yeshua spent most of His time with people who were ungodly sinners.

Perhaps you have set up a construct for yourself that you can only be in spaces with people who believe. But that leaves you without influence with people who don't believe what you believe. You lose the opportunity to shine the light of Yeshua in the darkness of this world because you cut yourself off. That's exactly what the Jewish leaders in John 5 were doing.

Some churches have signs that read, "Come as you are," often in combination with rainbow flags, to communicate that everyone is welcome there. It's important to understand, however, that in our context and from the Scriptures, you're supposed to come as you are but knowing that you'll have to change, because what you're doing with your life is not what God wants you to do with your life.

Although this is the message these signs are supposed to convey, sometimes you may feel like people need to work out their issues beforehand. Instead of doing as Yeshua says, you can be self-righteous about how good you truly are and expect people to change before they even step through the church doors.

Francis A. Schaeffer once said, "There is nothing more ugly than a Christian orthodoxy without understanding or without compassion."[71]

> Compassion asks us to go where it hurts, to enter into the places of pain, to share in brokenness, fear, confusion, and anguish. Compassion challenges you to cry out with those in misery, to mourn with those who are lonely, to weep with those in tears. Compassion requires you to be weak with the

weak, vulnerable with the vulnerable, and powerless with the powerless. Compassion means full immersion in the condition of being human.[72]

Proving to everyone how right you are is not a great goal. It can get ugly very quickly as you dismiss people's legitimate questions about Yeshua, God, and how faith works and just tell them to read the Bible for themselves. The Bible is a long book. I don't know about you, but I didn't read it once and go, "Oh, now I get it!" You have to keep reading it and keep studying it.

You need to find a better way to speak to people about these things. You need to encourage them and help them understand that you're not just concerned about their theology. Focusing solely on biblical orthodoxy at the expense of compassion drives people away from the church.

People who have had negative experiences with the church or religion or who have left their faith because it didn't make sense, or didn't speak into the practical issues of their lives, are going to ask you questions. They're going to want to share their stories and experiences. They might even want to hear what you have to say about it. For you to then tell them that they should just read the Bible and figure it out is not good enough. Don't tell people to change and then join us. Invite them to walk with you, and tell them that as they walk with you, you can figure these things out together—because you don't have all the answers either.

You do, however, know the God who has all the answers, and you're doing your best to follow Him. It's not easy, and there's a lot of pain, suffering, and hurt. People have to get through a lot before they even understand what's at the root of the questions they're asking. Far too often, we've just shoved the Bible in people's faces instead of engaging them in conversation.

Responding to God's Healing

Our passage in John 5 talks about the pool called Bethesda, perhaps better known as the pool of Bethesda. My family and I had the opportunity to visit the ruins of the pool of Bethesda in Jerusalem, and you can see layers when you look down into it, because Jerusalem has been rebuilt many times. Most of the places where you walk in Jerusalem are not where Yeshua would've walked because those places are many layers underground. In Yeshua's day, the pool would've been at ground level.

This site was excavated in the nineteenth century.[73] Prior to that, some commentators stated that John must have been taking some creative license with this story because there was no such thing as a five-sided pool in first-century Israel or Roman architecture. And then, archaeologists found it. You can argue all day about the truth of the words of Scripture, but you cannot argue whether these things happened or not, because the physical locations are there. You can argue to some degree about what happened at these locations, but you cannot say these people and places didn't exist, because they did and do. If you visit Jerusalem, you can see the pool of Bethesda, and it's one hundred percent clear that this is the pool described in John 5.

Verse 4, which explains why the pool of Bethesda was such a popular place for those seeking healing, does not appear in most translations since it's not in most of the earliest manuscripts. In the Tree of Life version, it's included as a footnote: "...because an angel of the Lord sometimes went to the pool and moved the water. Then, whoever went into the water first was healed from whatever disease he had" (John 5:4, footnote). It was certainly understood both in Jewish tradition and in Yeshua's day that this is what happened at the pool.

Verse 5 says that there was a man lying at the pool who had been an invalid for thirty-eight years. In verse 6, Yeshua asked him, "Do you want to get well?" I love how the man answered Yeshua, because he didn't say yes or no. Instead, he did what we often do when we're asked direct questions: he made excuses. He told Yeshua that he wasn't able to get into the pool when the water was moved, and other people always got in before he could.

Yeshua responded by telling the man to pick up his mat and walk. And amazingly, the man did. Anyone in the medical field can tell you that if someone has been lying down for thirty-eight years, there's no way they would be able to just get up and walk. Their muscles would've atrophied, to say nothing of the sores and infections they would've developed from lying down without moving for such a long period of time. It's an incredible, mind-boggling miracle.

All of this happened on the Sabbath. When this group of Jewish leaders saw the man walking around and carrying his mat, their first response was not to rejoice in his healing but to chastise him for carrying his mat on the Sabbath! This man was no newcomer; he had been lying at the pool of Bethesda for thirty-eight years. These leaders knew who he was. Yet that was their response to his healing, his restoration? "Sorry, buddy, but you can't be walking around and doing that kind of stuff today."

The former invalid explained that he was walking and carrying his mat because the man who had healed him told him to.

The Jewish leaders demanded to know who had healed him, but he didn't know, because Yeshua had slipped away into the crowd.

In verse 14, Yeshua found the man at the temple. This is important because, according to the Torah, the first thing you do after you've been healed is to go make sacrifices at the temple. The man clearly knew this, and the temple was only a short walk from the pool of Bethesda. Yeshua said to him, "Look, you've been healed! Stop sinning, so nothing worse happens to you!" (John 5:14b).

People have taken Yeshua's words here in all kinds of crazy directions. Was the man an invalid for thirty-eight years because of a sin he had committed? If he sinned again, would his legs stop working? It's really much more practical than that. Yeshua was saying, "Look, I just healed you. Don't use this opportunity to go and do whatever you want." Think about it. The man had been lying there for thirty-eight years. He was a grown man, and there were a whole lot of things he'd never done that he probably wanted to do. A lot of those would involve sin. Let's be real here: if nothing else, he was likely interested in finding a lady.

Yeshua was reminding him not to use his healing, the gift that God had given him, to commit sin. That's important for you to remember as well. Most of us have prayed a prayer like this: "God, I really need to pass this test. I'll give my whole life to You if You'll just help me pass this test." God helps you pass the test, but then you continue living as you always have.

You often make these commitments in hopes that God will help you in your difficulties, but when He does, you simply go back to your life and stop acknowledging Him. Yeshua, however, tells you to stop sinning, to use the gifts and the circumstances that God gives you for His glory and not for your own selfish, sinful purposes.

Building Fences Around the Law

One Sabbath, while my family and I were in Jerusalem, we saw an Orthodox Jewish neighborhood that had a barrier around it. In Orthodox Judaism, the rule is that you cannot do your regular work on Shabbat. This includes not carrying anything, so they've set up additional rules about what you can carry and what you can't—like how the man in John 5 wasn't allowed to carry his mat.

Then, they set up another rule that they could put a barrier around their neighborhood so that they can carry things on Shabbat within that neighborhood but not outside of it. It's easy to look at this and think, "Man, these guys are idiots. Who would do something like that?" but the truth is that you do this, too. You're just blinded to the fact that you're making up your own rules and living by those rules instead of by the actual Word of God. You shouldn't be so quick to judge their legalism while overlooking your own.

When believers find out I'm a Messianic rabbi, they tend to say something along the lines of, "That's so cool! I've always wanted to meet a Jewish person who believes in Jesus, but isn't it legalism to keep doing Jewish stuff? Isn't that Old Testament? Doesn't the New Testament tell us we don't have to do that Jewish stuff anymore?" To me, it's a funny assessment that Judaism was the old version, in which there was legalism, and Christianity is the new version, in which there is no legalism. Not exactly.

In Judaism, there's a concept called "building fences around the law." Take the commandment not to boil a calf in its mother's milk (Exodus 23:19), for example. Because Jewish people didn't want to break this commandment accidentally, they decided to separate dairy and meat products. They don't prepare meat and dairy together, they don't serve them together, and they don't eat them together. They put a fence around the law so that they wouldn't break the commandment by accident.

But then, a fence is put around that fence, and another fence is put around that fence. Eventually, there are ten fences around the original commandment, and after a few generations, no one remembers what the original commandment is. They just know they're not supposed to eat milk and meat at the same meal.

The problem is that nothing in the Torah forbids eating milk and meat at the same meal. In fact, in Genesis 18:8, Abraham broke that rule in the meal he prepared for God: "Then he took butter and milk and the young ox that he had prepared and set it before them. While he was standing by them under the tree, they ate."

This is the very reason why on Shavuot, which is traditionally a dairy-only holiday based on the same commandments, my family and I celebrate with a barbecue and make cheeseburgers. Based on what it says in Genesis 18:8, I'm pretty confident that Abraham served a cheeseburger to God.

The Christian version of building fences around the law is the concept of the slippery slope. The idea is that doing one thing will lead to another, and another, and the next thing you know, you've slipped and slid your way downhill and into sin. The best thing to do, therefore, is to never start that downward trajectory in the first place—to avoid doing the small things that have the potential to lead you into serious sin.

To give an example, let's say a single Christian is dating someone and they want to avoid sexual sin. They may decide that they aren't going to be alone with the person they're dating or that they aren't going to kiss the person they're dating until that person becomes their spouse. Nowhere in Scripture does it say that a boyfriend and girlfriend can't be alone together or that kissing is reserved for marriage, but some Christians see these as things that could lead them, personally, down the slippery slope into having sex before marriage. And so, they don't do them.

Building fences around the law and the slippery slope are not bad concepts in and of themselves. You're supposed to take precautions to keep yourself from sin. The place where they become bad is where the fences or the different points on the slope become commandments and you tell people that they have to do things "this way" so they won't sin. You tell them that they can't have that cheeseburger or that they can't kiss their boyfriend or girlfriend because it's against God's commandments.

Too often, you can focus on the letter of the law and not the spirit. You focus on what you do instead of why you do it, which is to honor God by keeping His commandments.

God has answered so many of your prayers and done so many things for you, yet you continue to do what you're doing. Yeshua comes to you in the same way that He came to that man, and He tells you, "Stop sinning." You use these fences and these points on the slippery slope to justify yourself and the logic behind why you do things, and that makes you feel good and secure and gives you a false sense of holiness. In reality, they're killing you inside because you're holding yourself to a standard that God never set and then holding other people to that same standard.

All along, however, God is reminding you that it's not that complicated: you just need to stop sinning. Scripture is clear about what constitutes sin. Paul even gave us a short list in 1 Corinthians:

> *Or don't you know that the unrighteous will not inherit the kingdom of God? Don't be deceived! The sexually immoral, idolaters, adulterers, those who practice homosexuality, thieves, the greedy, drunkards, slanderers, swindlers—none of these will inherit the kingdom of God. That is what some of you were—but you were washed, you were made holy, you were set right in the name of the Lord Yeshua the Messiah and by the Ruach[74] of our God.*
> **—1 Corinthians 6:9–11**

So, stop doing those things. Jesus did not end the observance of kosher laws for Jewish people.

The second of the seven "Rabbinic commandments" that Ronald Eisenberg says "were not based on a verse in the Torah" is called *netilat yadayim*. This is the general Hebrew term for ritual hand-washing, meaning lifting up of the hand. Though there might be some references in the Torah to washing, the codification of netilat yadayim in Orthodox Jewish practice happened late in Jewish history, with Maimonides' Mishneh Torah (twelfth century) and Joseph Karo's Shulchan Aruch (sixteenth century).

In Mark 7:5, the Pharisees approached Yeshua and His disciples with frustration: "Why don't Your disciples walk according to the tradition of the elders? Why do they eat bread with unwashed hands?" This "tradition of the elders" is probably the clearest example of traditions that the Pharisees believed and taught were commanded by God but, in fact, were not.

Again, this doesn't mean the tradition is bad. In fact, washing our hands, pots, pans, and utensils saved Jewish people from afflictions that affected other people groups around them. Infamously, Jewish people were blamed for the Black Death plague in the Middle Ages because their "attention to personal hygiene and diet, their forms of worship, and cycles of holidays were off-puttingly different."[75] But the simple fact was, "Jews regularly ritually washed and bathed, and their abodes were slightly cleaner than their Christian neighbors'. Consequently, when the rat and the flea brought the Black Death, Jews, with better hygiene, suffered less severely."[76] Turns out, washing is not a bad thing to do, a lesson we were reminded of during the COVID-19 pandemic. But it wasn't commanded by God; it was a "tradition of the elders." Let's look at the text here:

Now the Pharisees and some of the Torah scholars who had come from Jerusalem gathered around Yeshua. And they saw that some of His disciples were eating bread with unclean hands, that is, not washed. (For the Pharisees and all Jewish people do not eat unless they wash their hands up to the elbow, keeping the tradition of the elders. And when they come from the marketplace, they do not eat unless they perform a ritual washing. There are many other traditions they have received and hold, such as the washing of cups, pitchers, copper vessels.)

The Pharisees and Torah scholars questioned Yeshua, "Why don't Your disciples walk according to the tradition of the elders? Why do they eat bread with unwashed hands?"

And He said to them, "Rightly did Isaiah prophesy about you hypocrites, as it is written, 'This people honors Me with their lips but their heart is far from Me. And in vain they worship Me, teaching as doctrines the commandments of men.' Having left behind the commandment of God, you hold on to the tradition of men."

He was also telling them, "You set aside the commands of God, in order that you may validate your own tradition. For Moses said, 'Honor your father and your mother,' and, 'He who speaks evil of father or mother must be put to death.' But you say if anyone tells his father or mother, 'Whatever you might have gained from me is korban (that is, an offering to God),' then you no longer permit him to do anything for his father or mother, making void the word of God with your tradition that you've handed down. And you do many such things."

Then Yeshua called the crowd again and began saying to them, "Hear Me, everyone, and understand. There is nothing outside the man that can make him unholy by going into him. Rather, it is what comes out of the man that makes the man unholy."

When He had left the crowd and entered the house, His disciples questioned Him about the parable. And He said to them, "Are you then also lacking understanding? Don't you grasp that whatever goes into the man cannot make him unholy? For it does not enter into the heart but into the stomach, and then goes out into the sewer, cleansing all foods."

And He continued, "It is what comes out of the man that makes the man unholy. For from within, out of the heart of men, come evil intentions, sexual immorality, theft, murder, adultery, greed, wickedness, deceit, lustfulness, envy, slander, pride, and foolishness. All these evil things come from within and make the man unholy."

—*Mark 7:1–23*

This text is understood and taught by many Christians as the end of kosher (clean food) laws.

The website My Jewish Learning talks about the origins of natiylat yadayim: "The tradition of netilat yadayim prior to eating bread originated with the rabbis of the Talmud."[77] Note that Mark begins the narrative, "They saw that some of His disciples were eating bread with unclean hands, that is, not washed"

(Mark 7:2). The Talmud is the tradition of the elders, written down later. Remember, the Pharisees were the originators of the oral law.

My Jewish Learning continues regarding netilat yadayim: [78]

> It derives from various practices concerning ritual impurity from when the *ancient temple* stood in Jerusalem. The priests who performed the temple rituals were given gifts of oil, wine and wheat that could be eaten only after ritual washing. For various reasons, the ancient rabbis extended this practice to all Jews before eating meals. Some sources suggest that the practice was instituted so the temple's washing ritual would not be forgotten. Whatever the reason, the practice, incumbent upon both men and women, was established by Talmudic times and later included in the medieval codes of Jewish law. Some passages in the Talmud indicate that failing to wash hands before a meal is a significant transgression. *One Talmudic sage even says* that eating bread without washing is tantamount to having sex with a prostitute, while another says that acting contemptuously toward this ritual causes one to be uprooted from the world.

But Yeshua responded to the Pharisees' questions by quoting Isaiah: "Rightly did Isaiah prophesy about you hypocrites, as it is written, 'This people honors Me with their lips but their heart is far from Me. And in vain they worship Me, teaching as doctrines the commandments of men'" (Mark 7:6–7).

Watch the end of Yeshua's quote—"teaching as doctrines the commandments of men" (Mark 7:7b). At this point, you just have to pause and ask: what is the point of this story? Is it about the end of the list of unclean animals that God gave to the Jewish people? Or, like in Acts 10 (to which we will return in a later chapter), is God making a bigger point than what it seems at first glance?

I would suggest to you that food was not the point here for

Yeshua. It wasn't even the point for the Pharisees. Their point was that His disciples were not following the tradition of the elders. It wasn't about the Bible but about their traditions and man-made commandments, and Yeshua, by quoting Isaiah, pointed out that their hearts were far from God because they taught as "doctrines the commandments of men" (Mark 7:7b). Man, that must have been a tense scene!

You see, here—as in most of their interactions with Jesus— the Pharisees were arguing their own authority against His. They're like, "Who gave you the authority to not follow our rules?" Yeshua essentially replied, "I gave you the commandments in the first place, and no one gave you authority to add new ones that you created based on other things I commanded you." What I would give to have been there and watched it live (at the very least, on Facebook Live) so I could drop the meme of Michael Jackson in "Thriller," eating popcorn with the words, "I'm just here for the comments!"

Even today, Orthodox Judaism holds that if you don't wash your hands in the correct manner and say the correct blessing, then the kosher (clean) food you are about to eat becomes un-clean (non-kosher). The blessing, said in English, reads, "Blessed are you, O Lord, our God, King of the Universe, who has sanctified us through your commandments and has com-manded us concerning the washing of hands." There it is: the belief that "God commanded us concerning the washing of hands." But He didn't.

This is the reason Yeshua said the Pharisees made "void the word of God with your tradition that you've handed down. And you do many such things" (Mark 7:13). I do it, you do it, your pastor does it, your rabbi does it, Judaism does it, Christianity does it, men do it, women do it, parents do it, children do it.

You make void the Word of God with traditions you hand down and say they are from God. Need some examples? Try:

- Chick-Fil-A being closed on Sunday (cue Kanye, "you're my chick-fil-a").

- The old blue laws in New Jersey that kept stores closed on Sundays.

- Think about rules in evangelical denominations of Christianity regarding alcohol, card playing, and dancing. (We jokingly said at the Christian college I attended that we were not allowed to have premarital sex because it led to dancing. Don't you dare go down that slippery slope!)

Jesus was mad in Mark 7 because they had added a tradition of the elders to the actual commandments, then labeled it a commandment from God. It's like Yeshua was saying here, "I didn't command that—that's why I don't follow it!" In verse 15, He said it this way: "There is nothing outside the man that can make him unholy by going into him. Rather, it is what comes out of the man that makes the man unholy." Then follows, in verses 21–23:

> *It is what comes out of the man that makes the man unholy. For from within, out of the heart of men, come evil intentions, sexual immorality, theft, murder, adultery, greed, wickedness, deceit, lustfulness, envy, slander, pride, and foolishness. All these evil things come from within and make the man unholy.*

Well, dang, we all do those things! Jesus was saying your hands might be clean, you might never eat unclean food in your whole life, and yet, you will still be unclean because of what comes from the overflow of your heart. Which, of course, is not new, since it comes from Proverbs: "Guard your heart diligently, for from it flow the springs of life" (Proverbs 4:23). And from Ezekiel: "'As for those whose heart walks after the heart of their detestable things and abominations, I will bring their ways upon their heads.' It is a declaration of ADONAI Elohim" (Ezekiel 11:21). Yeshua repeated the same idea in the Gospel of Luke: "For from the overflow of the heart his mouth speaks" (Luke 6:45b). Same God, same message: "Your hearts are the problem, not My commandments."

We set up all of these justifications and get so stuck on them that people simply associate Judaism with legalism and believe that Jesus left Judaism to start a whole new religion. They think that when Jesus spoke, He was degrading the rabbis and all of Jewish history, telling them that He was starting over because they had messed it all up.

But really, none of us is any good at religion. You weren't designed to keep rules so that you can go to heaven. You were designed to recognize the One who formed you in your mother's womb and to follow Him with all your heart, with all your soul, and with all your strength.

Breaking Through Your Walls

"But, Rabbi Matt," you might be thinking, "there are so many people who don't do this. There are so many hypocrites in this world." Yes, and we are chief among them. Whether you use hypocrisy as an excuse not to turn to God or as an excuse for why the world is such an awful place, remember that you are not exempt from it.

Hypocrisy is like that. With so many hypocrites out there,

how can anyone do it right? There's One who did do it right. His name is Yeshua, and He is the One you must follow. Don't put your hope in people, in institutions, or in creeds or prayers that you've prayed. Beyond all these things is the God who makes promises and who goes to great lengths to keep these promises—and to prove to you that He is a keeper of His promises. He wants you to be someone who trusts in Him.

As we discussed previously, religious people say, "Change and you can join us," but Yeshua says, "Join us and you will change."[79] When those Jewish leaders saw the man who hadn't walked for thirty-eight years walking around and carrying his mat on the Sabbath (John 5:1–18), they should have responded with praise and celebration, not by bringing accusations against people who hadn't broken any of God's commandments.

Whenever I go on mission trips, I have been privileged to see all sorts of miracles happening right in front of my eyes. People are healed in the name of Yeshua. Maybe you're saying to yourself, "I want to stop sinning, but I can't stop doing this one thing." Here's the truth: you can. Not because you try really hard, but because God has given you everything you need to stop doing whatever is putting a wall between you and Him.

God wants you to break right through that wall, stop sinning, and acknowledge that He's the only One who can help you do it. He's the only One who can bring you the healing you need, who can speak the needed words of encouragement. He's the only One who can provide whatever you need.

You surround yourself with justifications, walls, hypocrisies, arguments, and excuses you believe are protecting you from being hurt or broken, but Yeshua reminds you that brokenness is where you're supposed to be. You're supposed to come to a point where you realize you can't do this on your own. And then, God says to you, "Now I can do something with you. Stand and walk."

You can do this because of who Yeshua is, not because of who you are, what you do, or the rules you set up for yourself. When you understand this clearly, you will stop judging others because they don't follow God exactly the way you do. Instead, you'll just love them for who they are. They're people who need Yeshua, just like you do, and He is the only fix for the issues they have in their lives.

You'll want as many opportunities as possible to speak into the lives of people who don't know Yeshua. People outright reject Him because of how He's been presented over the last two thousand years. That's a great place to start! So many people quote words they only *think* are scriptures, because they've heard people say these things and they've never actually opened the Bible to look at it for themselves.

Go back to the stories. Look at the Person He is, what He's done, and what He's calling you to do. The truth is, there's always something God wants to change in you. We love to make it clear to other people that God wants to change something in them. We tell them that they could be awesome if they would only let God change them. Just turn it around: "*I* could be awesome if *I* would just let God change *me*." You may be quick to judge everybody else while in the meantime, you're running away from what God wants to do inside of you.

So, stop sinning. Allow God to heal you. Allow Him to change your perspective and shift your worldview. Allow Him to help you see people the way He sees people. If you can get a hold of this concept for yourself as part of the family of God, I can see the family of God replete with all kinds of people who have hated God and rejected religion but who simply want to find the truth of God. I know this is possible, because I believe God is going to do more than we can hope or imagine (Ephesians 3:20). And that starts inside of us.

CHAPTER SIX

Jesus, the Jewish Messiah

Every culture has its own representation of Jesus. Beyond the ubiquitous white Jesus we see, there's a Jamaican Jesus, an Indian Jesus, a Chinese Jesus, and so on. People want to relate to Jesus, and in doing so, they make Him like themselves. This isn't necessarily a wrong or evil thing to do, but it's important to remember Jesus is Jewish. Trying to fit Him into one of our cultures, so to speak, removes the Jewish culture and background of Yeshua that Scripture maintains.

From Genesis to Revelation, the entire Bible is the story of God keeping His promises to the Jewish people. There isn't a Jewish Bible and a Christian Bible. However, many Christians have been taught that the Old Testament doesn't really matter as much as the New Testament. This has created a culture within the worldwide body of the Messiah that is biblically illiterate because they're not reading the Old Testament.

How can you say that the Old Testament is from God while also saying you don't really need it? Reading the New Testament is like trying to study higher-level math without knowing basic algebra. Without the context provided by the Old Testament, you cannot properly understand the New Testament.

Just like many Christians aren't reading the Old Testament and aren't understanding Jesus is Jewish, many Jewish people aren't reading the New Testament because they don't believe it's for them. In some cases, they even believe it's antisemitic— that it's against the Jewish people. Few are reading the entire story, which is meant to help us understand who Yeshua is. And part of that is understanding His Jewish background and culture.

Why Jesus' Jewishness Is So Important

When you strip Yeshua of who He was and is as a Jewish person, it's really hard to know Him. You can't understand someone without understanding their context. Some people think that means Christians should keep kosher and celebrate the Jewish holidays like Yeshua did, but that's not what I preach or what I subscribe to. I'm not trying to get all Gentiles who believe in Yeshua to live as though they're Jewish, but I do want everyone to understand Yeshua in His own Jewishness.

In his book *Restoring the Jewishness of the Gospel: A Message for Christians*, David H. Stern makes the case that you're not preaching the whole gospel—to Jews or Gentiles—if you're not preaching the Jewishness of Jesus.[80]

As Messianic Jews, we're not just trying to prove the Jewishness of Jesus so that Jewish people accept Him. We're also trying to help the nations understand that there's more to Jesus than what has been understood and that, over the past two thousand years, some things have been lost that were very much understood in the first century.

Part of Messianic Jewish theology is this idea that in our generation, God is bringing people back to the Jewishness of Jesus and helping them to understand His context. Judaism and Christianity have a complicated history together, but all of us need to come back to who Yeshua is.

Shmuley Boteach offers this insight about Christianity and the Jewishness of Yeshua: "From the very beginning, as Christianity branched away from Judaism to develop its own identity, Jesus was intentionally shorn of His Jewishness like Samson deprived of his strength. Christians obfuscated the idea of Jesus the Jew—preferring to see Him as an innovator, who transcended Judaism and brought it to a conclusion. This deception deeply alienated Jesus from the Jewish people and led to considerable torment and distress."[81]

However, the story of the Gospels is that Yeshua came to fulfill God's promises to the Jewish people, which He did. The only reason that there are any Gentiles who believe in Yeshua is that His Jewish disciples obeyed His command to share the gospel. By the way, this was not a new concept, either. God told the Jewish people several times in the book of Isaiah that we are a light to the nations (Isaiah 42:6, 49:6, 52:10, 60:3). That has always been our role in what God is doing, in whatever generation we're in, which is a tremendous honor!

God is helping the world to understand that now, even more than in the first century. Christians are reading the Bible in its entirety and realizing that what they've been told about the Old Testament doesn't really fit. They're beginning to realize that maybe Jesus didn't come to end Judaism or the Old Testament. Maybe He came for His people *and* for the people of every nation. It's a very exciting revelation!

Yeshua applies to every single culture as He is, and you

need to understand Him as He was—and is—so that you can worship Him in Spirit and in truth (John 4:23). To make Him out to be anything other than Jewish misses a crucial part of who He is.

Again, this doesn't mean that everyone who believes in Him becomes Jewish or that every Gentile who comes to Him needs to start doing Jewish things. This is not the goal. The goal is to recognize Yeshua for who He is and allow who He is to affect who you are.

When you understand who Yeshua is as fully man and fully God, it changes some of the things you're doing in your life as well as the way you understand God. It changes your relationship with Him and makes you a reader, a learner. You become someone who not only reads the Scriptures but also tries to understand them in their entirety.

The sixty-six books of what we know as the Bible span many centuries and cultures. It was written over a period of about fifteen hundred years by about forty different authors. Cultures rose and fell during that millennium and a half, and Jewish society underwent considerable changes. To understand the Old Testament, it's important to understand what was going on in the nation of Israel and to whom each author was speaking. Moses, Samuel, Jeremiah, Ezekiel, and Daniel all lived during different parts of Israel's history and spoke to different audiences about different issues.

It's the same in the New Testament. Paul spoke to certain issues because he was preaching the gospel to the Gentiles, while Peter and Jacob (James) addressed concerns brought forth by Jewish believers. The letter to the Hebrews is titled as such because it was written to Jews to answer Jewish questions, like how the sacrificial system, the priesthood, and the Temple were affected if Yeshua really was who He said He was.

Joseph Prefigured the Messiah

Over the centuries, the Christianized Yeshua has become someone the Jewish people cannot even recognize. His Jewishness has been stripped away, and He looks nothing like we would expect Him to look. And if He is truly the Messiah who was sent for us, why have so many of us suffered or even been killed in His name?

I recently had the opportunity to tour the Vatican in Rome, and while the history is amazing and the art fascinating, much of that very same art shaped the picture we all have in our head of what Jesus looked like. In Michelangelo's *Last Judgment* on the wall of the Sistine Chapel, Yeshua is a blond-haired, blue-eyed, short-haired, non-bearded man. A far cry from a nice Jewish boy who grew up in northern Israel.

The story of Joseph offers us some insight here. Let's take a look at Genesis 45, which is actually part of a Torah reading that goes with the seasons of Hanukkah and Christmas. To provide some background: Jacob had twelve sons, who became the patriarchs of the twelve tribes of Israel. Joseph was the second-youngest, and he was so favored by his father that his brothers became frustrated with him and sold him into slavery (Genesis 37).

At seventeen years old, Joseph was taken from his family, the beginnings of the people of Israel, and transported to Egypt. And yet, there's this wonderful statement that follows Joseph throughout every part of his life: "but ADONAI was with him." Take Genesis 39:2 for example: "But ADONAI was with Joseph.

So, he became a successful man in the house of his master, the Egyptian."

The overriding principle of Joseph's story is that God was still with him in Egypt, even though he was far away from his family, the things he had been taught, and the promises of God. Eventually, Joseph became second-in-command to Pharaoh. He warned Pharaoh about an impending famine in the land, and Egypt was able to prepare by storing up food. When the famine hit, people came from all over to get food from Egypt—including Joseph's brothers.

Scripture tells us that Joseph was thirty years old when Pharaoh made him second-in-command (Genesis 41:46). There were then seven years of abundance followed by seven years of famine. By the time Joseph's brothers came to him to purchase grain during the famine, Joseph had been in Egypt for at least twenty years. He had essentially become an Egyptian.

People might not have known Joseph was Jewish, because he looked like an Egyptian and spoke like an Egyptian. When his brothers first arrived, he spoke to them through a translator and pretended not to understand their language (Genesis 42:23). Joseph kept having to leave the room because he was overcome with emotion. Seeing the faces of his brothers who had sold him into slavery likely brought up anger as well as hope.

Benjamin wasn't with his brothers, so Joseph made a deal with them to go get Benjamin and come back. After seeing Benjamin, Joseph could no longer restrain himself and revealed who he really was.

Can you picture the scene? In his official capacity, Joseph would have looked similar to Pharaoh. He would have been wearing an elaborate headdress and ornate jewelry and seated on a throne decorated with Egyptian symbols of power. His brothers would have been trembling before him. And then, this powerful Egyptian ruler had a meltdown.

> *Now Joseph could no longer restrain himself in front of all those who were standing by him, so he cried out, "Get everyone away from me!" So, no one stood with him when Joseph made himself known to his brothers. But he gave his voice to weeping so that the Egyptians heard, and Pharaoh's household heard. Joseph said to his brothers, "I am Joseph! Is my father still alive?" And his brothers were unable to answer him because they were terrified at his presence.*
> **—Genesis 45:1–3**

Imagine how his brothers must have felt. This Egyptian official had already put them in jail and somehow thought they had stolen from him, and now he was revealing that he was the brother they had sold into slavery. What on earth were they supposed to do?

Joseph then made an incredible speech:

> *Then Joseph said to his brothers, "Please come near me." So, they came near. "I'm Joseph, your brother—the one you sold to Egypt," he said. "So now, don't be grieved and don't be angry in your own eyes that you sold me here—since it was for preserving life that God sent me here before you. For there has been two years of famine in the land, and there will be five more years yet with no plowing or harvesting. But God sent me ahead of you to ensure a remnant in the land and to keep you alive for a great escape. So now, it wasn't you, you didn't send me here, but God! And He made me as a father to Pharaoh, lord over his whole house and ruler over the entire land of Egypt."*
> **—Genesis 45:4–8**

Can you imagine the guilt Joseph's brothers felt? They knew what they had done to their brother, and they knew how much grief they had brought to their father. Yet Joseph stood there in front of them and said, "It wasn't your fault. It's okay. I forgive you." They must've been waiting for the hammer to drop. Instead, Joseph made them (in my best Godfather voice) an offer they couldn't refuse:

> *Go up quickly to my father and say to him, "Thus says your son, Joseph: God has made me lord over all Egypt. Come down to me. Don't delay. Then you'll live in the land of Goshen, and be close to me, you and your children and your children's children, your flocks and your cattle, and everything that belongs to you. I'll provide food for you there— for the famine will last another five years—otherwise you'll lose everything, you and your household, and everything that belongs to you." And look, you and my brother Benjamin can see with your own eyes that it's my mouth that's speaking to you. You must tell my father about all my honor in Egypt, and about all that you've seen. And you must quickly bring my father down here.*
> *—Genesis 45:9–13*

Goshen, by the way, was where the Jewish people were living when Moses came to set us free.

Joseph's speech concludes with Genesis 45:14–15: "Then he fell upon his brother Benjamin's neck and wept while Benjamin wept upon his neck, and he kissed all his brothers and wept upon them. Finally, after this, his brothers talked with him."

Such an incredible moment! All of this was thrust unexpectedly upon the brothers, as this Egyptian spoke to them in Hebrew, told them that he was their brother whom they had sold into slavery, and assured them that everything was okay because God had done this and, now, he was going to save all of them.

This is why it's so important that all believers understand Jesus as a Jew. In the same way Joseph's brothers found it difficult to accept who Joseph was and that he was going to save them, with everything that has been done to the Jewish people in the name of Jesus over the last two thousand years, it is so hard for us to believe this is the Messiah who was sent for us.

Just as Joseph was a Hebrew who looked like an Egyptian yet promised salvation to the Jewish people, Yeshua—however He may look in people's minds—reveals Himself as the Jewish Messiah. "I am Yeshua HaMashiach, (Yeshua, the Jewish Messiah)," He says, "and I have come for My people so that they might recognize who I am, and so My brothers might worship Me the same way Joseph's brothers worshiped Him. I know all the pain. I was there in the Holocaust, and I was there in the pogroms, and I was there every time the Jewish people were kicked out of a country in My name. I was there, and I'm here now, and I'm speaking in the language of My people. I am one of you, and I have come to save you."

First for the Jew, and Also for the Greek

Please understand that Jews are not more important than the other nations. However, it is important to put Jesus in His proper context, because the Jewish people need to recognize Him for who He is first so that we can fulfill our role as a light to the nations. This is the part God has given us to play, and this is what God is doing in Messianic Judaism in this generation.

God has given me and others a voice in this moment in history. It's a burden that we don't want to bear on our own. It has nothing to do with who we are and everything to do with who He is. It is because of what He is doing in this generation to help all people who call upon the name of Jesus to understand Him as a Jew. The goal is not for everyone to become Jewish but for everyone to become followers of the Jewish Messiah.

Christian leaders like Pastor Robert Morris are not just understanding this truth but are also putting it into action. At his church, Gateway Church in Dallas, they added a Shabbat service on the first Friday of every month. The service serves as a Jewish expression within the church to preach the gospel to Jewish people and also to give Jewish followers of Jesus who attend Gateway a place to express their Jewishness in Yeshua.

John 3:16 explains God's purpose in sending Jesus to earth: "For God so loved the world that He gave His one and only Son, that whoever believes in Him shall not perish but have eternal life." There is an order, however, in how God is doing this.

An important verse in many Messianic congregations, reads, "For I am not ashamed of the Good News, for it is the power of God for salvation to everyone who trusts—to the Jew first and also to the Greek" (Romans 1:16). Many people tend to put a mental period after the word trusts, as the gospel is indeed for everyone, but Paul made it clear that the gospel goes to the Jewish people *first* and then also to the people of every nation. It's a message for the Jewish people first, but it's also a message to everyone from every part of the world. This has always been the heart of God.

Some people will ask, "Then why would God allow all these awful things to happen to the Jewish people? Why would He allow there to be so many obstacles between Jews and their Messiah?" I don't know the answer to those questions, but I do know with certainty that God promised never to leave or forsake the Jewish people, and He has kept that promise.

Six million Jewish people were murdered in the Holocaust.[82] Do you realize, however, that the Jewish population is almost back to the numbers before the Holocaust? The Hittites, the Jebusites, and the Canaanites are all long gone, but we are still here, and we continue to grow in number. Again, to be clear, this is not a celebration of who we are but of who God is.

Here's the truth: Yeshua is the God of Israel. He's the God of Abraham, the God of Isaac, and the God of Jacob. He is the God who was there with Joseph throughout his story. Yeshua was there all along—He has no beginning and no end (Hebrews 7:3). He is the visible image of the invisible God (Colossians 1:15).

He was born into this world as a baby and lived thirty-three years. In the last three years of His life, Yeshua ministered all over Israel, and many Jewish people became His followers. He died during Passover, rose from the dead during Passover, and ascended into heaven forty days after Passover. Then, on the day of Shavuot, the day we celebrate the giving of the Torah, God gave His Spirit to Jewish people who were gathered at the temple in Jerusalem, because they were supposed to be there to receive the Spirit of God in the same way and with all the same imagery that accompanied Moses on the mountain on that very same day.

All these things are deeply connected to each other, and when you take Jesus out of His Jewish context, when you don't talk about His Jewishness, you miss who He is and what He came to do. He came for the Jewish people so that He could also come for everyone from every nation who calls on His name—whatever that name might be in their language.

Wrestling with Your Faith

The mission of the Messianic synagogue where I serve as rabbi is to lead people to become fully devoted followers of Yeshua, and our first core value is to reflect His Jewishness. My wife and I had been married for sixteen years when we first put up a Christmas tree. She has wonderful memories of Christmas as a child, so why not?

I posted a picture of our Christmas tree on social media, and I got all kinds of digital dirty looks from people in the Messianic community and from people who already have Christmas trees. There isn't one right answer for everyone as to how we should do these things. We're wrestling through the history of God redeeming the people of Israel so that He could redeem the world, and as we do so, we're putting the "messy" in Messianic.

The more you read and the more you learn, the more questions you're supposed to have. We must wrestle with the Scriptures as a community so that we can find Yeshua in the midst of it all. You find the person of Yeshua and what He's called you to do, which is to be like Him in mercy and grace, compassion and longsuffering. And in His suffering, He thought about you. You're supposed to do the same for the people around you when you are suffering. There are so many simple things that we lose when we don't understand the Jewishness of our Messiah—who He was, and still is, and what He came to do.

Yeshua invites us to so much more than we could ever hope or imagine, because it's about Him, not us. It's about the revelation of who He is and what He's called us to—to be able to say to the people around us, "I know Him. I have a relationship with Him, and I could introduce Him to you."

You can overcomplicate your faith so much that you lose your focus on what you're actually called to do, which is to tell people that there is only one God and His name is Yeshua. He is the God of Abraham, Isaac, and Jacob. He is the God who has always been, and He has never changed.

He sent His Son to die for the sins of the world and offered Himself as a sacrifice so that you and I could find the freedom to which He's calling all of us—not just for our sakes but so that we can lead others to that same freedom as well. It really is that simple.

And yet, you have to wrestle with these things. It's the difference between the Bible and all other books. The Bible has the ability to speak to you in every season of your life, every day, over and over again as you read the same words. Every time I read Scripture, I find something new. It doesn't make any sense, because the words are the same as they've always been, but God is constantly speaking to us through them. He wants you to understand who He is so that you can be a person who is "not ashamed of the Good News, for it is the power of God for salvation to everyone who trusts—to the Jew first and also to the Greek" (Romans 1:16).

If you have not accepted Yeshua as Messiah, I encourage you to ask Him to introduce Himself to you. You can say something like, "I don't know if I agree with every word of what I just read, but if You're real, I want to know You." Don't pray this unless you actually want Him to show up, however—because He's going to!

If you already are a believer, please know that you can be reintroduced to Yeshua every day. If you're wrestling with something in this season, you can say something like, "Lord, I need You to prove Yourself to me. I need You to show up. I need You to do something in my life. I need You to transform me."

Again, you need to be careful when you pray that prayer, because it's going to hurt. God is going to change things in you that you didn't expect Him to change. I know there are certain things on your mind you'd like Him to fix, but He's going to fix things in your life that you're not even aware of right now.

The more you can do this with the Lord, the more the Spirit of God will radically transform your life. You will then be able to show others how they, too, can be radically transformed.

CHAPTER SEVEN

The Jewishness of Communion

To understand Yeshua in His original Jewish context, you must understand the last two thousand years of history since He came, as well as some of the thousands of years before He came. I am not trying to dismiss the rabbis entirely, and neither am I trying to dismiss the church fathers entirely. My goal is to bring together all the messiness and pain of family, theology, and people's journeys into faith so that you may become a better and more fully devoted follower of Yeshua.

The Scriptures show that if you understand Yeshua in His Jewishness, you will get what you need from His story. You will understand the mission and the purpose that He has for your life, whether you are Jewish like Yeshua or are a non-Jewish person who calls on the name of the Jewish Messiah.

Communion is a Jewish rite that has been adopted and adapted by Christianity. It's celebrated in all different kinds of churches all over the world, but it has distinctly Jewish origins. To better understand the concept of communion, you need to have a better understanding of its Jewish context. Let's take a look at one of the passages in Scripture that pertains to this.

Eat My Flesh and Drink My Blood

John 6:22–70, when Jesus referred to Himself as "the bread of life," took place long before Yeshua had His last Passover—which you may also know as the Last Supper. In this passage, Yeshua was having a conversation with a crowd of people, that likely included some Jewish leaders, about who He was and what He came to do. Let's jump to John 6:53–58:

> *So Yeshua said to them, "Amen, amen I tell you, unless you eat the flesh of the Son of Man and drink His blood, you have no life in yourselves. He who eats My flesh and drinks My blood has eternal life, and I will raise him up on the last day. For My flesh is real food and My blood is real drink. He who eats My flesh and drinks My blood abides in Me, and I in him. Just as the living Father sent Me and I live because of the Father, so the one who eats of Me will also live because of Me. This is the bread that came down from heaven—not like the bread your fathers ate and then died. He who eats this bread will live forever."*

If you want to lose disciples, tell them to eat your flesh or drink your blood. That's what happened to Yeshua: "So when many of His disciples heard this, they said, 'This is a hard teaching. Who can listen to it?'" (John 6:60). To translate: "What the heck is this guy talking about?

Remember, this conversation wasn't taking place in the context of the Passover. Here, the people were talking about how the children of Israel were in the wilderness and God sent manna from heaven to feed them, and they demanded that Yeshua perform a similar miracle to prove He was who He said He was (John 6:30–31).

Yeshua responded that God was giving them the true bread

from heaven: "For the bread of God is the One coming down from heaven and giving life to the world" (John 6:33). Of course, the people clamored for this bread, and Yeshua told them He was the bread of life. That's wasn't exactly what they were expecting to hear. Yeshua further explained:

> *Amen, amen I tell you, he who believes has eternal life. I am the bread of life. Your fathers ate the manna in the desert, yet they died. This is the bread that comes down from heaven, so that one may eat and not die. I am the living bread, which came down from heaven. If anyone eats this bread, he will live forever. This bread is My flesh, which I will give for the life of the world.*
>
> *—John 6:47–51*

This was, as we've already established, a hard teaching for the people to hear. Verse 61 continues, "But Yeshua knew His disciples were murmuring, so He said to them, 'Does this offend you?'" I love that Yeshua owned that moment.

Peter is my favorite person in the New Testament because he took things to extremes. He was either all in or all out. Even though he didn't really understand what Yeshua was talking about, there was no way he was leaving Him. "Simon Peter answered Him, 'Lord, to whom shall we go? You have the words of eternal life! We have trusted and have come to know that you are the Holy One of God'" (John 6:68–69).

Others, however, were not so committed. Verse 66 tells us, "From this time, many of His disciples left and quit walking with Him." Prior to this, Yeshua had chosen twelve disciples, which included Peter. As He taught, He gained other disciples who also left their families and their towns so they could literally follow Yeshua. Wherever Yeshua would stop for the night, they would set up camp and sleep, and wherever Yeshua would stop to teach, they would sit and listen.

Right before this, in John 6:1–15, Yeshua performed a miracle by multiplying five loaves of bread and two fish so that they fed five thousand people. These disciples would've witnessed this miracle and would have been the ones distributing the food to the people. So it wasn't that a few people got upset with Him and left. A number of people, people who had left everything behind to follow this rabbi, left and quit walking with Yeshua.

More Than Bread and Wine

It is from these verses in John 6 that we get all these different theologies about communion that exist within the spectrum of Christianity. Transubstantiation is, according to the teaching of the Catholic Church, "the change of the whole substance of bread into the substance of the Body of Christ and of the whole substance of wine into the substance of his Blood. This change is brought about in the eucharistic prayer through the efficacy of the word of Christ and by the action of the Holy Spirit. However, the outward characteristics of bread and wine, that is the 'eucharistic species', remain unaltered."[83]

The Lutherans do not believe the bread and wine literally become the flesh and blood of Yeshua, but they do believe there's a presence of Yeshua within the bread and wine (consubstantiation).[84]

Reformed Christians, such as Calvinists, do not believe the bread and wine are actually Yeshua's flesh and blood, but they believe a spiritual nourishment occurs when they partake of the Lord's Supper; more specifically, it is given to seal the promise that those who partake of the bread and wine in faith truly partake of the body and blood of Christ. Calvin explains this in terms of the believer's mystical union with Christ. Just as baptism is connected with the believer's initiation into union with Christ, the Lord's Supper strengthens the believer's ongoing union with Christ.[85] And the Plymouth brethren considered Communion to be simply a symbolic reenactment of the Last Supper.[86]

Christians generally don't see anything strange about eating Jesus' body and drinking His blood, but it becomes a lot more complicated when you're Jewish. Leviticus 17:10–12, which is in the Torah, is pretty clear on the matter:

> *Anyone from the house of Israel, or from the outsiders dwelling among them, who eats any kind of blood, I will set my face against that soul—the one who eats blood—and will cut him off from among his people. For the life of the creature is in the blood, and I have given it to you on the altar to make atonement for your lives—for it is the blood that makes atonement because of the life. Therefore, I have said to Bnei-Yisrael: No person among you may eat blood, nor may any outsider dwelling among you eat blood.*

God had instituted a sacrificial system of sacrificing bulls, goats, or doves, depending on income. Sacrifice was also a big part of the worship of the pagan religions that surrounded the Jewish people, and they would drink the blood of their offerings, whether the offerings were animals or humans. God therefore created this rule about drinking blood to separate His people from the nations.

He made it clear that when we sinned, we were to make an animal sacrifice. The life of the animal was in its blood, and atonement would come from the blood when it was spilled on the altar. We were not to drink the blood, because the blood was meant to make atonement for our sin and bring us forgiveness and redemption.

When Yeshua told His disciples to eat His flesh and drink His blood, those verses from Leviticus would have been on their minds. They were confused, and maybe even appalled, because they knew they were not supposed to do those things. This was a moment, however, where if a person knew what they were supposed to know about the Scriptures, they would have come to the conclusion that Yeshua was speaking metaphorically.

His body would be sacrificed for the sins of the world to restore our fellowship with God, and His blood would be poured out to make atonement for our sins. Instead of the temporary atonement secured by the blood of animal sacrifices, Yeshua's blood would atone for our sins permanently. By accepting Yeshua's sacrifice on our behalf—that is, eating His flesh and drinking His blood—we are able to have eternal life.

Although some of Yeshua's disciples walked away from Him because of this issue, it made all of His disciples wrestle with who Yeshua was and what He came to do. It's only in the last five hundred years that Christian believers have begun to realize Yeshua was speaking metaphorically.

The Origins of the Lord's Supper

Somewhere along the line, the Jewish context of these and other scriptures was done away with through the belief that Yeshua had fulfilled everything. This is where language can get a little tricky. For many people, fulfilling something means to bring it to an end, so they teach Yeshua "ended" ancient Judaism and its associated practices and started Christianity and the church. They see a dividing line between what is old and what is new, but that doesn't fit with the continuity of the whole story of what God is doing.

God established in the Torah that the life of a creature is in its blood. And it is because of the Torah, and because of who Yeshua is, that the sacrifice of His blood for us is so important. Although some of Yeshua's disciples were confused by Yeshua's invitation to eat His flesh and drink His blood, for the most part, they wouldn't have thought He was speaking literally. Since this conversation took place before the Passover, it didn't make a lot of sense at the time. Once the Passover arrived, Yeshua gave His disciples a more detailed explanation.

One of the oldest accounts of the body and the blood is in Paul's first letter to the Corinthians, which was written before the Gospels were written down.[87] The congregation in Corinth was not celebrating what Paul called "the Lord's Supper" with the proper respect. He described what the Lord's Supper commemorates, in 1 Corinthians 11:23–26:

> For I received from the Lord what I also passed on to you— that the Lord Yeshua, on the night He was betrayed, took matzah; and when He had given thanks, He broke it and said, "This is My body, which is for you. Do this in memory of Me." In the same way, He also took the cup, after supper, saying, "This cup is the new covenant in My blood. Do this, as often as you drink it, in memory of Me." For as often as you eat this bread and drink this cup, you proclaim the Lord's death until He comes.

Earlier in the letter, Paul described how the Corinthian believers were eating together but neglecting each other (1 Corinthians 11:22). For Paul and for the disciples, the Lord's Supper
wasn't a small piece of bread and a little sip of wine. It was a
meal they shared when they gathered together to teach the
Scriptures and share the teachings of the apostles. The bread
and the wine were incorporated into the meal, and it was all part
of the celebration.

The Corinthian believers were apparently coming into the
service to eat and drink without even considering why the bread
and wine were there in the first place. Paul had to correct them,
explaining that when they gathered together, they were supposed to care for each other. Some of them were eating at home,
and some of them were getting drunk before they came. They
needed to understand the importance of the Lord's Supper and
that it was to be done in remembrance of Him.

Still, the Lord's Supper is not a replacement of things that
came before. It's a continuation. In Judaism, we have the Kiddush, which is a blessing over the wine,[88] and the Hamotzi,
which is a blessing over the bread.[89] These blessings predate
Yeshua's time on earth both in the Scriptures and in Jewish tradition.

In 1 Corinthians 11:26, Paul uses the phrase, "as often as
you eat this bread and drink this cup," which some people interpret as meaning we should celebrate the Lord's Supper often.
But that's not what Paul was communicating. He was referring
to the Kiddush and the Hamotzi, which are recited over the
wine and the bread every Friday night for the start of Shabbat.
Judaism had already been doing this for a very long time.

In Judaism, both in the Scriptures and in tradition, wine is considered a celebration of life, because wine brings joy. During times of celebration, people bring out the stuff they can't afford to drink on regular days. Some families save their good wine for Friday nights, the start of Shabbat, because Shabbat is a day separated from the other six days. It's the seventh day. It stands alone, so in a moment of joy, we celebrate the wine and all that God has given us.

Bread, in Jewish tradition, is a sign of sustenance. You need bread to live. It's a symbol of life. The blessings over the wine and bread would not only be done at the start of Shabbat but also at the synagogue. If you eat a meal in the afternoon on Saturday, you'd do the blessings again. Wine is then used again in the Havdalah, the blessings that close the Shabbat on Saturday night.[90] All these things are part of the celebration.

When Paul said to the Corinthian believers, "as often as you eat this bread and drink this cup" (1 Corinthians 11:26), there was already an "often" even for the Gentiles because they had learned from the Jewish people. Accordingly, they celebrated these same things in similar ways.

Why Do We Do What We Do?

When non-Jewish people come to a Messianic congregation like mine, they often ask why we don't do communion. I explain some of the things we've discussed in this chapter, and that settles the issue for many people. Others, however, still want to do communion the way they've always done communion. They want to stick with the traditions they grew up with.

Most people want to keep their traditions relating to the holidays of Christmas and Hanukkah, because they like the warm, fuzzy feeling their traditions give them. They want their kids to have that same feeling. That's why people who do not believe in God at all still celebrate Christmas, Hanukkah, and Passover. But these same traditions can move you away from what the Scriptures are actually telling you to do. You have to take a step back and ask yourself why you do what you do, not only with the holidays but with communion as well.

I get frustrated as I write about this because I've read so many "Messianic" articles that rail against the church and against history. They say we should abandon this tradition or that tradition because they have pagan origins and we shouldn't do pagan things, but they remove all the good that has come out of some of those traditions. It's so much easier to point my finger at you and say, "You're doing it wrong," than it is to point my finger back at myself and ask the question, "Why do I even do the things that I do? Why do I even care about the things that I care about?"

There's nothing wrong with doing communion the way churches do it, but it's important to recognize that it's been taken out of the Jewish context in which it was created. It's become a totally non-Jewish event.

Jesus didn't come on the scene and say, "I've got this crazy idea. We are going to take this wine, we are going to bless it, and then we're all going to drink it together. And then, we're going to do the same with the bread. From this point forward, when you do these new things that we've created, you're going to think of Me." These things already existed in Jewish tradition.

A Blessing That Predates
Yeshua's Life on Earth

In fact, the first place wine and bread show up together is in Genesis 14, when Melchizedek came to see Abraham. We know very little about Melchizedek. His name in Hebrew translates to "king" and "righteous," which is why he was both a king and a priest (Genesis 14:18–19). Melchizedek served Abraham bread and wine and blessed him, and Abraham then gave Melchizedek a tenth of the plunder he acquired in battle. The book of Hebrews states that Yeshua is a priest forever according to the order of Melchizedek (Hebrews 5:6), which leads some of us to believe that Melchizedek was actually a preincarnate Yeshua.

One of the reasons for this conclusion is the exchange between Yeshua and the Judean leaders, when He said: "'Your father Abraham rejoiced to see My day; he saw it and was thrilled.' Then the Judeans said to Him, 'You're not even fifty years old and you've seen Abraham?' Yeshua answered, 'Amen, amen I tell you, before Abraham was, I am!'" (John 8:56–58). Some of the people got mad at Yeshua and tried to stone Him because He called Himself God. But Yeshua was saying, "You don't understand. Abraham knows Me, and I know Him because I was there with him. We shared bread and wine together as part of a celebration of who I am and what I was going to do."

According to Genesis 14:18–20, Melchizedek brought out the bread and wine and blessed Abraham. This likely would have included the Hamotzi, which we mentioned earlier is the traditional Jewish blessing over the bread. It goes, "Baruch Atah Adonai Eloheinu melekh haolam hamotzi lechem min haaretz." In English, this means, "Blessed are You, Lord God, King of the universe, who has given us bread from the earth."

Since the text simply says that Melchizedek "blessed" Abraham (Genesis 14:19), if you're not familiar with the Hamotzi, you wouldn't know that it's the blessing he would have said. If you understand the Jewish context of the Scriptures, you know that this traditional blessing would have been recited. It existed before Yeshua's time on earth, and Yeshua's disciples would do it in remembrance of Him, not dismissing what had come before.

According to the *Jewish Encyclopedia* entry on the Kiddush, "from the controversies between the schools of Shammai and Hillel on various points connected with the Kiddush, it is clearly seen that the ceremony is very old."[91] Shammai and Hillel were two rabbis who taught during the first century B.C. They argued over just about everything and came to different conclusions, so you would've followed either Shammai or Hillel. We therefore know for a fact that the Kiddush was performed in the first century B.C., prior to Yeshua's birth. The bread and wine would've been part of every celebration Yeshua and His family ever celebrated. It's part of all the holidays. It's part of Shabbat.

Remembering and Honoring
What Has Come Before

I also did some research on Christian perspectives on communion. Michael H. Jenkins' article on bread and wine as religious symbols states, "Jesus' actions reflect Jewish tradition, in that he blessed both [the bread and wine] and distributed them to the assembled. However, breaking with Jewish tradition, Jesus explains the bread and wine as a symbol of his own body and blood, and thus his sacrifice to redeem the world."[92]

This seemed to be the general Christian understanding: that Jesus broke with Jewish tradition and created His own. But that's not actually what happened—there was no breaking of tradition.

On Shabbat, we celebrate the wine for joy, and we celebrate the sustenance that comes from bread. On Passover, we celebrate the Passover lamb with the blood that was put on the doorpost of our houses, and we celebrate unleavened bread. Outside of Passover, we celebrate leavened bread to remember the Exodus from Egypt, when God freed us from four hundred years of slavery because He had promised Abraham He would send a deliverer to set us free.

By saying the bread was His flesh and the wine was His blood, Yeshua was not breaking with Jewish tradition. He was saying, "As you have already done these things to remember what has been done for you, so you will now do these things to remember Me." In fact, He was right in step with Jewish tradition. As the Messiah, He had the right to add to the reasons why we celebrate with bread and wine, but He didn't abrogate the things that came before. He simply said, "As often as you do this, now do this also in remembrance of Me." And that's how Paul interpreted it in 1 Corinthians.

When my family and I celebrate Shabbat and do the blessings over the bread and wine, we also add, "We break the bread as Yeshua's body was broken for us." We remember Yeshua, but we are also grateful for Shabbat and for the Exodus and for everything God has done for His people.

In his article "Ten Things You Should Know about the Lord's Supper and Communion," Sam Storms writes, "[Communion] is a personal remembrance. We are to remember Jesus. The focus isn't on Abraham or Moses or Isaiah. The focus is no longer on the Jewish Passover or the night of His betrayal or anything else. The focus is Jesus. 'Do this in remembrance of me.'"[93]

What's funny about statements like that is that communion is supposed to be a remembrance of all those things. When we do these celebrations, we're supposed to acknowledge all the things God has done for anyone who calls on the name of Yeshua in the course of human history—because He set up a whole system so that when Yeshua came and died, it would make sense to the Jewish people and He would set us free from our sins. He will set anyone free who calls on the name of Yeshua and believes in the sacrifice that He made for us.

It's easy to say, "All you need to do is focus on Jesus," but when you focus on Jesus, you need to understand His Jewish context. Everything He did came from Judaism. Anyone who views communion as a "personal remembrance" should consider attending a Passover Seder.

For centuries, rabbis have taught that when we celebrate the Passover, we remember the Passover as if we were personally there. The Passover is not just something that happened in history. This is something we participated in personally. As we remember the Exodus, we also remember the sacrifice that Yeshua made for us.

This brings us to Luke 22, which describes what many people know as "the Last Supper." It was actually a Passover Seder meal that Yeshua was sharing with His disciples—the same meal that all Jewish people have during the Passover. Again, if you've never attended a Passover Seder, I highly recommend you do, as it will help you to better understand what Yeshua and His disciples were doing.

> *And when He had taken matzah and offered the bracha, He broke it and gave it to them, saying, "This is My body, given for you. Do this in memory of Me." In the same way, He took the cup after the meal, saying, "This cup is the new covenant in My blood, which is poured out for you."*
> —**Luke 22:19–20**

The word *bracha* in verse 19 refers to a blessing.[94] Once again, Yeshua would have recited the Hamotzi to bless the bread and the Kiddush to bless the wine. This was an amazing moment where Yeshua was not inventing something new but tying together all of Jewish history for the people who were sitting at the table with Him and for everyone who would read it from that point on.

Just as God set us free from slavery in Egypt, so does He want to set us free from our slavery to sin. Just as we were saved by the blood of the Passover lamb that was put on the doorposts, so we are saved by the blood of Yeshua, our Passover Lamb, our Messiah who spilled His blood so that we could have the forgiveness of sin. For the life of the creature is in its blood, and that's where atonement comes from. There's a price that has to be paid, and Yeshua paid that price for us.

The "New Covenant"

Yeshua told His disciples that this cup was the new covenant in His blood (Luke 22:20). This is the only place where Yeshua talked about the new covenant, and the term "new covenant" wasn't even new when He used it.

People do all kinds of funny things with the term "new covenant." They make it mean you no longer need the old covenant, just the new one. But you can't understand the new covenant without understanding the old covenant.

Yeshua was referring to Jeremiah 31:30 when he talked about the new covenant: "'Behold, days are coming'—it is a declaration of ADONAI—'when I will make a new covenant with the house of Israel and with the house of Judah.'" All of the Jewish people who heard Him talk about the new covenant would have known He was quoting Jeremiah.

This new covenant was between the house of Israel, which was the northern kingdom, and the house of Judah, which was the southern kingdom. Together, these two kingdoms made up the Jewish people. It goes on to say about the new covenant:

> "...not like covenant I made with their fathers in the day I took them by the hand to bring them out of the land of Egypt. For they broke My covenant, though I was a husband to them." It is a declaration of ADONAI. "But this is the covenant I will make with the house of Israel after those days"— it is a declaration of ADONAI—"I will put My Torah within them. Yes, I will write it on their heart. I will be their God and they will be My people."
> —*Jeremiah 31:31–32*

When Yeshua lifted the cup and said, "This cup is the new covenant in My blood" (Luke 22:20), it was therefore just like all the other covenants with the Jewish people.

God made a covenant with Abraham:

> I will richly bless you and bountifully multiply your seed like the stars of heaven, and like the sand that is on the seashore, and your seed will possess the gate of his enemies. In your

seed all the nations of the earth will be blessed—because you obeyed My voice.

—Genesis 22:17–18

God also made a covenant with Israel through Moses that the Jewish people would obey His commands (Exodus 19–24). Very rarely in the history of Israel did we obey God, but the way God handles covenants is that He doesn't break His end even when we break ours. He made a promise to never leave us or forsake us (Deuteronomy 31:6).

In fact, back in Jeremiah 31:35–36, God said:

"Only if this fixed order departs from before Me"—it is a declaration of ADONAI—"then also might Israel's offspring cease from being a nation before Me—for all time." Thus says ADONAI: "Only if heaven above can be measured and the foundations of the earth searched out beneath, then also I will cast off the offspring of Israel—for all they have done." It is a declaration of ADONAI.

We all break covenants. It is God's grace and mercy that He doesn't break His covenants based on what we do. If God has abandoned or replaced the Jewish people, then no person from any nation has any hope. If He did that to us, then He will do that to you, too. But He hasn't left us, and He will not leave you. We are proof that He does not leave the people with whom He makes covenants.

Yeshua came along, and He fulfilled the Abrahamic and Mosaic covenants. He was the son of Abraham. He was an Israelite who kept the commandments perfectly. There is one more covenant that precedes what we call the new covenant, which is the Davidic covenant. God made a covenant with David, King of Israel, that a son of David would come who would rule forever (2 Samuel 7:12–16). Being descended from the house of David (Matthew 1:1–17), Yeshua fulfilled this covenant as well. Scripture tells us that He sits at the right hand of the Father on the throne as the son of David (Matthew 22:41–46).

Yeshua is this amazing Person who, being fully human and fully God at the same time, came and met all the requirements of each of the covenants that have come before, and His intent is to bless the whole earth. He is the son of Israel, and though we can't keep the covenants perfectly, He did. It's what made Him a kosher sacrifice when He offered Himself for our sins.

Joining in the Celebration

We are to continue the traditions that predate Yeshua, and that He participated in and encouraged us to do in remembrance of Him. God Himself in the Person of Yeshua kept all the covenants on our behalf so that He could keep the promises He made to the whole world.

When Chabad, the ultra-Orthodox Jewish organization, quotes from the Talmud regarding the Messiah and the wine, it says, "We celebrate the Sabbath as a testimony to God having created the world in six days and resting on the seventh and at that time he set aside special wine to be used at the celebratory meal when the Messiah comes."[95]

There is celebratory wine for the celebration of when the Messiah—and this is exactly what Yeshua was doing when He stood up at Passover—lifted the cup, said the blessing with His disciples, and inaugurated the new covenant. This covenant was first for the Jewish people but also for anyone from any nation who calls on the name of Yeshua.

When we eat His flesh and drink His blood, we are not doing it physically. We are not breaking the Torah by drinking blood. We are using it as a metaphor to understand the great sacrifice that Yeshua made for us.

I believe there is a day yet coming when we will celebrate the wedding banquet of the Lamb (Revelation 19:9). Yeshua will gather the entire body of Messiah—all the people who believe in Him and follow Him as His bride—and He will stand up with the special wine. He will lift the cup, and He will recite the Kiddush: "Blessed are You, Lord our God, King of the universe, who has given us the fruit of the vine" so that we can celebrate all that God has done for anyone from any nation who calls on the name of Yeshua.

When you take the bread and the wine, pause to remember all that God has done for you even though you are a covenant-breaker who continues to sin. God is not up there shaking His head over the fact that you don't have your act together; He is inviting you into the celebration.

You don't have to live in the pain and agony that comes from living apart from His presence. You can live in God's presence, know Him, and walk with Him. He is the One who formed you in your mother's womb, and He has a great plan and purpose for your life—more than you could ever imagine from where you are right now. But you have to trust in the One who did all of these things, and as often as you do them, do them in remembrance of Him.

CHAPTER EIGHT

The Jewishness of Baptism

When you hear the word *baptism*, many things come to mind. I've found that people believe John the Baptist was the first person to perform baptisms. They think of him as telling people to fold their arms and hold their nose and then dunking them in the river while saying, "In the name of the Father, the Son, and the Holy Spirit."

Depending on which Christian tradition a person belongs to, they might think of baptism as being dunked fully in the water or having water sprinkled on you or having water poured over your head three times. When you go back to Judaism and the Torah—where baptism actually comes from—you find that the Hebrew word translated as *baptism* means "immersion," which means baptism is a full immersion in the water.[96]

The terms *baptize* and *baptism* now have Christian theological connotations that may color an attempt to understand the biblical concepts described using words for washing or immersion, like βαπτίζω (*baptizō*). The Greek words typically translated *baptism* in the New Testament, such as βάπτισμα (*bap-*

tisma), should not be regarded as technical terms for the Christian practice. To avoid unnecessary confusion with the contemporary Christian concept of baptism, the relevant Greek words may accurately be translated as *immersion* (*baptisma*; *baptismos*) and *immerse* (*baptizō*).

The Purpose of Immersion

There are all sorts of things in the Torah that have to do with purifying ourselves before God. The mikveh is a ceremonial bath used for ritual purification. When a woman has finished her menstrual cycle, she goes into a mikveh and cleanses herself because that's what Scripture commands her to do (Leviticus 15:19–30). Likewise, when a man has a seminal emission, he goes into a mikveh to cleanse himself (Leviticus 15:16). Both the woman and the man have to make themselves clean because they have been made unclean.

The Torah is very specific about what God says is clean and what He says is unclean. God tells the Jewish people that everyone else is unclean but that you are to be clean, so you need to follow these rules to be made clean.

Recall how, in the Middle Ages, the Jewish people were blamed for the Black Death. Since they weren't getting sick, some people thought they had put a curse on the people who did get sick. The truth is, however, that the Jewish people washed their dishes, washed their hands, and kept their bodies clean. It was a perfect recipe for avoiding the plague and many other diseases (shout out to COVID-19). Historically, cleanliness has been viewed differently in Judaism than by other religions or people-groups.

Matthew 3 says that John the Baptist invited people to repent of their sins and be immersed by him in the Jordan River. If you've participated in any kind of baptism before, you likely picture John as holding the person being baptized—while they fold their arms and hold their nose—and dunking them in the water before bringing them back up. In reality, John was most likely standing there while people were walking into the river and dunking themselves.

Though he was called John the Baptist, he wasn't a Baptist. He did not start the Baptist Church. That came much later in history. Like the Essenes, a sect of Judaism in the first century, John lived in the wilderness. He "wore clothing from camel's hair and a leather belt around his waist, and his food was locusts and wild honey" (Matthew 3:4). John was kind of a weird guy.

What confuses people is that John preached immersion for repentance and the forgiveness of sins. They think it was a new thing—that this concept was not found in the Torah—but the reason you immerse yourself in a mikveh is because you are repenting for your sins, or your uncleanness. You are asking God to forgive you and make you clean again, and He does. John was essentially running a mikveh. Just as with most things that happened in the New Testament, there was a context that the Jewish people who saw it and heard it would have understood.

At the time, some people thought John was the Messiah because there was an expectation that the Messiah would immerse people for the forgiveness of their sins. That was why John clarified that he was not the Messiah but the one who comes before the Messiah by saying, "I am 'the voice of one crying in the wilderness, "Make straight the way of ADONAI," as the prophet Isaiah said'" (John 1:23).

All of these things made sense to the Jewish people who were standing there listening. When you remove the context of these Jewish things and try to make them into brand-new things that are unrelated to the things that came before, you miss all that was happening.

John 3:22–30 records what happened when Yeshua began immersing people in the same area as John:

> *Afterwards, Yeshua and His disciples came to the land of Judea. There He was staying with them and immersing. Now John also was immersing at Aenon near Salim, because much water was there and many were coming and being immersed; for John had not yet been thrown into prison. Now an argument came up between John's disciples and a Judean concerning purification. They came to John and said, "Rabbi, the One who was with you beyond the Jordan, the One you testified about—look, He is immersing, and all are coming to Him!" John answered, "A man can receive nothing unless it has been given to him from heaven. You yourselves testify that I said, 'I am not the Messiah,' but rather, 'I am sent before Him.' The one who has the bride is the bridegroom, but the best man rejoices when he stands and hears the bridegroom's voice. So now my joy is complete! He must increase, while I must decrease."*

This took place after John immersed Yeshua—or, more accurately, after Yeshua immersed Himself under John's supervision (Matthew 3:13–17). Yeshua and His disciples then began immersing people further up the Jordan River.

I love this moment because John's disciples, who had been following him for some time, took note of this and basically said to John, "Hey, we're trying to build a ministry here. We're doing great things, and we're seeing money come in from different places. Maybe we'll be able to buy a building one day. But now this guy has started a new congregation a few minutes up the road, and people are going to Him instead of you. What are we supposed to do?"

And John replied, "Guys, He's the One we were talking about. You were there when I immersed Him in the Jordan. Remember the voice that came from heaven and said, 'This is My Son, with whom I am well pleased' (Matthew 3:17)? I'm the guy before the guy. He's the guy. He's the One we've been waiting for."

Baptism of the Holy Spirit

Take note of John 3:25 in this passage: "Now an argument came up between John's disciples and a Judean concerning purification." This is how Jewish people communicate. We argue first, and then we come to some kind of conclusion. This argument would've been about who is supposed to be immersed and how and when, and this wouldn't have been the first time this conversation happened. The old adage is, in every conversation with two Jews, there will be at least three opinions.

In the nation of Israel, many ancient mikvehs have been found because immersion was such a common ritual. One example is in the city of Ein Kerem, believed by some to be the home of John. *Haaretz*, an Israel magazine, published an article in 2015 about a family that found a large mikveh under their home.[97]

People being immersed in water was also a common practice at the Temple as part of the sacrificial system. If you visit the southern wall of the Temple Mount, you can walk into mikvehs from the first century. They most certainly were used by Yeshua and His disciples, because they were used by everyone in the first century who would make sacrifices at the Temple.

Immersion in water or baptism was very common in the first century. Immersion was also connected to different views on whether Gentiles could become Jews through conversion. This conversion could include immersion as well as circumcision. In order to understand this we have to dig into the book of Acts and the relationship between Jews and the first Gentile followers of Yeshua.

It is believed that the events in Acts 2 happened in A.D. 30, the same year as Yeshua's resurrection only fifty days later. Acts 10, around A.D. 40, is the story of Peter sharing the gospel with an uncircumcised Gentile, a Roman centurion, and how the Holy Spirit fell on him and those in his household as it had the Jewish disciples ten years earlier.[98] When the Holy Spirit filled these Gentiles, Peter's response was to immerse them in water.

Acts 15 is about a council in Jerusalem, around A.D. 49, where the Jewish disciples of Yeshua argued over what Gentiles must do to be granted repentance and follow Yeshua.[99] Did they have to become Jews? Become circumcised? Should they be immersed in water? A period of about twenty years passed, following the Resurrection, before the apostles came to a conclusion about whether a Gentile could even follow Yeshua.

Birth of the Church

Many Christian preachers call Acts 2 the birth of the church as the new people of God—a replacement of the Jewish people, although still including Jewish people who followed Jesus. Charles Ryrie wrote that "Pentecost marks the beginning of the church as a functioning body by the outpouring of the Spirit on that day."[100] D. S. Dockery said, "The church was inaugurated at Pentecost (Acts 2) as God's new society."[101] The *Encyclopedia of the Bible* notes, "Just as the original people of God were called to proclaim God's mighty acts of deliverance (Isaiah 43:20, 21 Greek OT), so the new people of God are called to 'declare the wonderful deeds of him who called you out of darkness into his marvelous light' (1 Peter 2:9)."[102]

So according to these theologians, when the first Jewish followers of Yeshua were filled with the Holy Spirit—in the Temple courts, in Jerusalem, on the day of Shavuot, with Peter preaching in Hebrew and only Jewish people from every nation hearing Peter preaching in their own language—somehow, this movement became a brand-new, non-Jewish people of God. Or the Holy Spirit of Jesus Christ created a New Israel called the Church of Jesus Christ, which "occupies the place in the new covenant that Israel occupied in the old. Whereas in the Old Testament the kingdom of God was peopled by national Israel, in the New Testament it is peopled by the church."[103] Well, that doesn't sound very Jewish, does it?

In reality, nothing new happened in Acts chapter 2 (that rhymes for memorizing purposes). Shavuot, according to Jewish tradition, is also the day Moses received the Torah on Mt. Sinai. The disciples therefore understood that what happened to them in Acts 2 was equal in importance to what had happened on Mt. Sinai. Not new, not better, not a mulligan, not a move away from Jewish people or national Israel, but rather, the fulfillment of God's promises to the Jewish people that opened the doors for Gentiles to come to Yeshua. Acts 2 is not about the start of the church; it's about the hope of Israel being made known to the Jewish people in the person of Yeshua so that we, Jewish people, could fulfill our mandate to make Yeshua known to the Gentiles.

The original Jewish followers of Yeshua could have never imagined Yeshua being identified as something other the Jewish Messiah who practiced Judaism and whom they followed as their Rabbi. Flip that over to the present day, when I, as a Jewish follower of Jesus, am told on a semi-regular basis, in person and on the internet, that Jews "don't" or "can't" believe in Jesus. But it seems the original followers of Yeshua wondered if it was possible for Gentiles to follow Jesus since followers of Jesus—at least for the first ten years after Yeshua's death and resurrection—were almost exclusively Jewish. And it would take another ten years before the Jewish apostles figured out what a Gentile following the Jewish Messiah would even look like.

Again, that's ten to twenty years when Jesus was followed almost exclusively by Jews. So, how did Gentles begin to join this Jesus movement? This is a good spot to take a break from reading this book and check out the biblical narrative yourself. It's cool, I'll wait for you to read the first nine chapters of Acts, recorded by the Gospel writer Luke.

Just in case you're short on time, here are some cheat codes for you: up, up, down, down, left, right, left, right, B, A, start (that's for old school Nintendo kids). As Yeshua was leaving, ascending into heaven, He said in Acts 1:8, "But you will receive power when the Ruach ha-Kodesh [Holy Spirit] has come upon you; and you will be My witnesses in Jerusalem, and through all Judah, and Samaria, and to the end of the earth." Tim Mackie of the Bible Project notes that the whole book of Acts follows a similar pattern:[104] the telling of the story after Jesus' resurrection began in Jerusalem (chapters 2–7), moved to Judea and Samaria (8–12), and then ended in Rome, with Paul's mission to the Gentiles (nations), or the "ends of the earth" (13–28).

All of this means that the original Jewish disciples of Yeshua fulfilled their commission by Yeshua, because they very literally preached the gospel in Jerusalem, Judea, Samaria, and the ends of the earth. They set a pattern in preaching the gospel that is first for Jewish people and then also for the nations, and it is a pattern missing in most congregations in the world that follow Jesus. It's the same pattern Paul followed when he wrote to the congregations in Rome, "For I am not ashamed of the gospel, for it is the power of God for salvation to everyone who believes, to the Jew first and also to the Greek" (Romans 1:16).

Where Are the Gentiles?

Acts 2 includes a mention of "proselytes" among Jewish people in Jerusalem for Shavuot, known by most Christians as Pentecost. *Shavuot* in Hebrew means "weeks" (a reference to the counting of seven weeks—49 days + 1—commanded to Israel following Passover in Leviticus 23:15–16). *Pentecost*, from Greek, means "fifty days," a similar reference. When the Holy Spirit was poured out in Acts 2, it was only given to Jewish people and those connected to Jewish people, known as proselytes or God-fearers.

Acts 2:5 says, "Now Jewish people were staying in Jerusalem, devout men from every nation under heaven." Then Luke listed where those Jewish people were from, in Acts 2:9–11:

Parthians and Medes and Elamites and those living in Mesopotamia, Judea and Cappadocia, Pontus and Asia, Phrygia and Pamphylia, Egypt and parts of Libya toward Cyrene, and visitors from Rome (both Jewish people and proselytes), Cretans and Arabs—we hear them declaring in our own tongues the mighty deeds of God!

The only mention of Gentiles here is "proselytes," and the rest were Jews from other countries or regions. These proselytes were counted as Jews because they observed all the same things as Jewish people.

The next place where Gentiles perhaps show up in Acts is in chapter 8, when Philip went to Samaria (Acts 8:5). It says, "Philip went down to the main city of Samaria and proclaimed the Messiah to them." The origin of the Samaritans is debated in different circles, but it is commonly understood that "Samaritans were despised by Jews, on account of their intermarriage with Gentiles after the fall of the northern kingdom in 721 B.C."[105] At the same time, Samaritans "were not regarded as Gentiles by the Jews, but as part of the lost sheep of the house of Israel."[106] The *Lexham Bible Dictionary* notes that Samaritans were a "group of people who believed they were the true descendants of Israel and keepers of the Torah."[107]

That brings us to the Ethiopian eunuch. Acts 8:27–28 says, "So he got up and went. And behold, an Ethiopian eunuch—an official who was responsible for all the treasure of Candace, queen of the Ethiopians—had traveled to Jerusalem to worship and was now returning. Sitting in his chariot, he was reading the prophet Isaiah." While some consider this man not to be Jewish, you have to consider a few things.

First, there is a long history of Ethiopian Jews that dates back to the time of Solomon and the Queen of Sheba. Second, he "traveled to Jerusalem to worship and … was reading the prophet Isaiah." Because he was traveling to Jerusalem to worship and reading a Jewish prophet, there is a high probability that he was Jewish, or at the very least a God-fearer with connection to the Jewish people. Unlike today, Gentiles did not travel to Jerusalem to worship the God of Israel while reading

Isaiah.

In Acts 10, Cornelius, a Roman soldier and God-fearer (Gentile connected to Judaism), was the first non-Jew to be immersed in the name of Yeshua, along with those in his house. As the book of Acts tells the story, up until this point, only Jewish people were coming to faith in Yeshua and being immersed in His name. By the end of this story, when retold by Peter in Acts 11, there was astonishment by the Jewish apostles in Jerusalem. After hearing Peter's account, they "glorified God, saying, 'Then even to the Gentiles God has granted repentance leading to life!'" (Acts 11:18).

Which was a weird response. Why didn't they understand that "God has granted repentance leading to life" even to Gentiles? Because at this point, it was their earthly experience that God only saved Jewish people. That the Holy Spirit only fell on Jewish people. But Peter saw the Holy Spirit fall on Gentiles and told the apostles that "the Ruach ha-Kodesh fell on them, just as on us at the beginning" (Acts 11:15).

Them: Gentiles. Us: Jews. Same Holy Spirit! Christian commentaries make this passage sound like God wanted to end kosher (purity) laws. For example, that "the early church had to solve the problem of kosher food laws in order to launch a mission to the Gentiles. Purity distinctions and human discrimination are of a single piece."[108] Or, "the old purity laws could no longer separate Jew from Gentile. Since God had shown himself no respecter of persons, neither could Peter be one anymore."[109] Or, "removal of dietary restrictions would imply a freedom to associate with Gentiles and therefore prepare the way for a legitimate Gentile mission."[110]

Not so fast! The Second Temple period was dominated by the rules of the Pharisees when it came to daily life. In fact, it was commonplace in the time of Yeshua for Jewish people not to eat with Gentiles and to separate themselves from Gentiles in many ways. It seems that God used something Peter, as a Jew, would never do—eating unclean food—to help him understand that Gentiles were not unclean.

After all, when Peter arrived at Cornelius' house, he said, "You yourselves know that it is not permitted for a Jewish man to associate with a non-Jew or to visit him. Yet God has shown me that I should call no one unholy or unclean" (Acts 10:28). Look in the Torah: there is no such law. So, what was Peter talking about?

Here is how the logic goes: God told Jewish people not to eat animals He called unclean (think, the list in Leviticus 11). If Jews eat those animals, they become unclean. Gentiles eat those animals, so they must be unclean. If Gentiles are unclean because of the animals they eat and Jews are clean by not eating those same animals, then Jews should not associate with Gentiles so as to not become unclean. In the same logic of Gus Portokalos—the dad in *My Big Fat Greek Wedding* who makes the root of every word Greek—"and there you go!"[111]

For this reason, it was common in the first century for Jews not to associate with Gentiles because of the differences in food. David H. Stern writes:[112]

> It is not difficult to find evidence in Jewish sources for what these Gentiles were "well aware" of, that although nothing in Jewish law says that Gentiles themselves are common or unclean, many of their products and practices were regarded as conveying ritual impurity or were for other reasons forbidden to Jews. At one point the Mishna says, straightforwardly, *"The dwelling-places of Gentiles [literally, 'Canaanites,' meaning Gentiles in the Land of Israel] are ritually unclean" (Ohalot 18:7).*

In fact, today, modern Jewish orthodoxy is not much different. Jeffery Spitzer, a teacher of the Bible, Rabbinics, and Jewish history at the American Hebrew Academy, writes:[113]

> *Jewish law tries to separate Jews from gentiles, in order to prevent Jews from adopting idolatrous behaviors. Extensions of the dietary laws limited social interactions. Jews are not allowed to leave their wine with idolaters, lest it be used for idolatry (Shulhan Arukh Yoreh Deah 128:1), and food cooked by non-Jews is also prohibited (Yoreh Deah 113:1ff.). There are exceptions and loopholes, but the general force is to discourage interaction between Jews and non-Jews.*

When Peter said, "You yourselves know that it is not permitted for a Jewish man to associate with a non-Jew or to visit him" (Acts 10:28), he was not talking about the Torah, as there is no commandment for such a separation. Instead, as Robert Wall puts it, Peter "confirms God's plan to allow uncircumcised but repentant Gentiles to experience the blessings of Israel's salvation and defines the terms of Paul's future mission to the Gentiles."[114]

Separation is a principle for understanding how we as Jews live and act, and how our understanding of what is clean and unclean affects our daily decisions. God set apart a people, the Jewish people, for Himself, but His purpose was to open the doors wide for anyone, from any nation, who calls on the name of Yeshua. This is not new, as it was God's plan all along back to the covenant He had made with Abraham that "in you all the families of the earth will be blessed" (Genesis 12:3).

So, what Peter actually learned, in his own words, was,

"God has shown me that I should call no one unholy or unclean" (Acts 10:28). And then, in his explanation to the other Jewish apostles, he said, "Therefore if God gave them the same gift as also to us after we put our trust in the Lord Messiah Yeshua, who was I to stand in God's way?" (Acts 11:17).

David H. Stern notes:[115]

> *If Jewish law made Gentile products and practices unclean, it would have been only human, all too human, for people to have extended the description, "unclean," to Gentiles themselves. Such attitudes would have been not so much taught as caught, absorbed from the total milieu; and the influence of these attitudes would have quickly become pervasive. This is why it took direct intervention from God to shake Kefa [Peter] loose from them.*

Peter had Cornelius and those in his house immersed in water, and for the first time in history, Gentiles were brought into the family and promises of God with a confession of faith and immersion in water—not as converts to Judaism, but as full members without becoming Jews.

In the New Testament, as we've seen, after the death and resurrection of Yeshua, there was about a twenty-year period when only Jews were being filled with the Holy Spirit and coming to faith in Yeshua.[116] From the Resurrection to Acts 10, when Cornelius became the first Gentile immersed in water for the forgiveness of his sins, only Jewish people were coming to faith. When God instructed Peter to go to Cornelius, lead him to the Lord, and immerse him in water, the big question all of the Jewish disciples were asking was, "Is this allowed?" Their experience as Jews involved only immersing Jews, because in their experience, only Jewish people were responding to the gospel.

To Convert or Not Convert?

It was a Jewish belief that the Messiah would come, and it fit within a Jewish context. It was all centered on Judaism. Once Paul began preaching to the Gentiles, however, the Jewish disciples had to address the issue of how to receive Gentiles. Should they all convert to Judaism and become Jewish?

Toby Janicki, from First Fruits of Zion, writes in his book on the Didache, a late first-century document believed to be written by the apostles, that "the origins of immersion practices in the early believing community were firmly rooted in the Judaism of the Second Temple Period."[117] There is a discussion in the Talmud, Yevamot 46a and 46b, regarding conversion of Gentiles to Judaism. At the end of the discussion, the rabbis decide that converts must be circumcised and immersed in water. But there is an alternate opinion that a convert only had to be immersed.

The arguments regarding conversion were happening during the first century within all of Judaism. When Yeshua, His disciples, and Paul said that all Gentiles needed to do was immerse themselves in water, they were choosing a side in the Jewish argument. They took it one step further and said that Gentiles didn't need to convert to Judaism at all.

Acts 15 is generally known as the Jerusalem council because the meeting was in Jerusalem. Technically, it was at least the second such meeting in Jerusalem, because Peter had gathered the same apostles in Acts 11 to recount his experience with Cornelius.

The account of this Jerusalem council begins by noting that "some men coming down from Judea were teaching the brothers, 'Unless you are circumcised according to the custom of Moses, you cannot be saved'" (Acts 15:1). A few verses later, we find that these "brothers" were also Pharisees: "But some belonging to the party of the Pharisees who had believed stood up, saying, 'It is necessary to circumcise them and to command them to keep the Torah of Moses'" (Acts 15:5).

Christian commentaries make this out to be a "scandalous" event. Ajith Fernando writes, "If Paul preached circumcision, there would be no scandal to Christianity. But since he preached that salvation occurs through no work of our own and only through the merits of the death of Christ, such a message was scandalous to the average Jew. The teachers from Judea were trying to remove this scandal."[118]

But because of Peter and Cornelius, it was hardly scandalous, and the average Jew would understand, in the first century, that there were varying opinions of what conversion to Judaism would involve for a Gentile. For some, like these Pharisees who seem to be followers of Yeshua, that would include circumcision. For others, like Peter in Acts 10, only immersion in water.

Again, this was a common argument in all of Judaism, found even in the Talmud (Yevamot 46a).[119] Barker and Kohlenberger write, "Paul's new policy for reaching Gentiles, despite his claim of the authority of revelation and of providence for it, seemed to many Jewish Christians to undercut the basis of ministry of the Jerusalem church."[120] But it was not Paul's "new policy," as he followed Peter's lead, and it was not undercutting fellow believers in Jerusalem.

The very reason for the council was that in light of Peter and Cornelius, and because of the work of Paul and Barnabas in

Antioch among Gentiles, the apostles needed to make a clear decision. This is why, after discussion from Yeshua-following Pharisees, Peter, Paul (also a Pharisee), and Barnabas, Jacob (James) then stood up, quoted Amos, and said, "Therefore, I judge not to trouble those from among the Gentiles who are turning to God" (Acts 15:19), subsequently identifying four prohibitions (categories, really) that Gentiles ought to keep.

These four prohibitions were not new, either, "because each has biblical warrant and constitutes a requirement imposed on non-Israelites in the OT [Old Testament]."[121] In a footnote of this quote, Carl Holladay writes, "'Aliens residing among Israelites' are prohibited from sacrificing to other gods (Leviticus 17:8–9), from eating blood (17:10, 12–13), and probably, though not certainly, from eating meat of improperly slaughtered animals (17:8–9)."[122] With that in mind, there was no scandal at the Jerusalem council; it was a decision that would be considered among normative practice for Gentiles connected to Jewish life and practice in the first century.

Let's pause for a second on Jacob, whom most know as James. The change in name, although not seemingly intentional, was the doing of John Wycliff, in the first translation of the Bible in English in the fourteenth century, when the Greek name Iakōbos was translated as *James*. In 1611, The King James Version kept *James* in honor of King James I, who commissioned the translation for use in the Anglican Church.

The problem, writes Mark Wilson, is that "James's ancestral lineage is lost.... In Matthew's genealogy, we learn that Joseph's father was named Jacob (Matthew 1:16) and that his family tree included the patriarch Jacob (Matthew 1:2). James was thus named after his grandfather."[123]

This is one of many instances where important Jewish fig-
ures in the New Testament were stripped of their Jewishness.
Jacob is important because he was the brother of Yeshua, the
leader of the congregation in Jerusalem, and the one who then
presided over this important council in Acts 15. It's why he had
the authority to say, in verse 19, "Therefore, I judge." But Jacob's judgment wasn't new; it was a Holy Spirit-filled understanding (twenty years after these Jewish men first received the
Holy Spirit) of the words Jacob quoted from the prophet Amos.
So Jacob said, "Therefore, I judge not to trouble those from
among the Gentiles who are turning to God" (Acts 15:19).

David Hoffbrand, in his book *The Jewish Jesus*, says that
"the apostles realized that if God wasn't requiring the Gentiles
to convert or to follow all His commandments before accepting
them, then neither should they. So, finally, they sent a letter to
this effect, making the position clear to everyone—Gentiles remain Gentiles as believers."[124]

In the following verses, the apostles sent Paul and Barnabas,
along with Judah and Silas, with the letter to Antioch, where
"the disciples were first called "Christianoi" (Acts 11:26). The
Jewish disciples were called Christians in Antioch because they
were Jews who followed the Christ.

Here, being called "Christians" was not a separation from
them being Jewish. It was an identifier of what kind of Jews
they were: Jews who followed the One they believed was the
Messiah. *Christian* means "follower of Christ," and *Christ* is
the Greek word for the Hebrew word *Messiah*. Both words,
Christ and *Messiah*, mean "anointed one." That's why these
Jews were called Christians.

In Acts 21, Paul and Jacob (I know, it's confusing, James)
had a conversation related to these issues.

When we arrived in Jerusalem, the brothers and sisters welcomed us gladly. On the next day, Paul went in with us to Jacob; all the elders were present. After greeting them, he reported to them in detail what God had done among the Gentiles through his service. And when they heard, they began glorifying God.

They said, "You see, brother, how many myriads there are among the Jewish people who have believed—and they are all zealous for the Torah. They have been told about you—that you teach all the Jewish people among the Gentiles to forsake Moses, telling them not to circumcise their children or to walk according to the customs. What's to be done then? No doubt they will hear that you have come.

"So do what we tell you. We have four men who have a vow on themselves. Take them and purify yourself along with them and pay their expenses, so that they may shave their heads. That way, all will realize there is nothing to the things they have been told about you, but that you yourself walk in an orderly manner, keeping the Torah.

"As for Gentiles who have believed, however, we have written by letter what we decided—for them to abstain from what is offered to idols, and from blood, and from what is strangled, and from immorality."

The next day Paul took the men, purifying himself along with them. He went into the Temple, announcing when the days of purification would be completed and the sacrifice would be offered for each one of them.

—*Acts 21:17–26*

First, take note of Jacob's statement that there were "many myriads ... among the Jewish people who have believed—and ... are all zealous for the Torah" (Acts 21:20). Including the apostles, there were many Jewish people who continued to keep the Torah and follow Yeshua. But Jacob's concern was an accusation against Paul that he was teaching "all Jewish people among the Gentiles to forsake Moses, telling them not to circumcise their children or walk according to the customs" (Acts 21:21).

Paul, with Jacob's encouragement, went to the Temple to "purify himself" and pay for the same purification for other Jewish believers. This action was proof to other Jewish believers that Paul and Jacob both believed Jewish people should continue to circumcise our sons, but that Gentiles do not share the obligation to circumcise their sons or convert to Judaism through circumcision.

Furthermore, Paul wrote letters to two young men to whom he referred as "sons" in faith in Yeshua. The first, Timothy, was Jewish through his mother but was never circumcised because his father was Greek. The second, Titus, was a Greek with no Jewish ancestry. Two "sons," yet with Timothy, being Jewish, Paul himself "took him and circumcised him for the sake of the Jewish people in those places—for they all knew that his father was Greek" (Acts 16:3). Whereas, with Titus, Paul celebrated in Galatians that "yet not even Titus who was with me, a Greek, was forced to be circumcised" (Galatians 2:3). The simple difference being that one was Jewish and the other was not.

This position fits the narrative in Acts 21, where both Jacob (you get it by now, James) and Paul agreed that Jewish followers of Yeshua ought to continue to circumcise their sons but Gentiles, consistent with the teaching of the apostles, did not share the same obligation. In reality, Gentiles never did share the same obligation and still, today, do not.

In college, one of my professors announced, "I did not have my son circumcised, to prove he was free from the law." This thinking is a part of the problem we are addressing in this book.

Jewish people aren't *trying* to be free from law. It's the constitution of the Jewish people. We keep commandments because God loved us first and we, in turn, show our love for Him by doing what He commanded us to do. To my Gentile professor, my question is: Why would you try to prove that you are free from something you were never under in the first place?

There is no commandment in the Torah for Gentiles to be circumcised other than during the first Passover celebration (Exodus 12:44, 48). But this was about leaving Egypt, prior to the Jewish people making a covenant with God at Mt. Sinai through Moses. It was never repeated as a lasting commandment for Gentiles, and the disciples, along with other normative Jewish viewpoints in the first century, never made it a requirement for Gentiles turning to Yeshua. While Jewish followers of Yeshua continued both circumcision and immersion in water as identifiers, it was immersion in water (not circumcision) that became the normative practice of outward identification for Gentiles turning to the God of Israel, like Cornelius in Acts 10.

Gentiles are immersed into the forgiveness of their sins, and in believing in Yeshua and being immersed, they are grafted into Israel and all the promises are theirs as Gentiles. The truth is, all you need is to believe that Yeshua is the Messiah. After believing that Yeshua is the Messiah, you are immersed in water as a sign that you are standing with God and God is standing with you.

The Origin of Infant Baptism

Then, we come to this curious scripture in Colossians 2, which has been wildly misunderstood for thousands of years.

Keep in mind that Paul was writing to a mostly Gentile audience in the city of Colossae. The congregation was started by his disciple Epaphras, and we don't have any record of Paul visiting the Colossian congregation personally.

Epaphras visited Paul while he was under house arrest in Rome and told him about the faithfulness of these Gentile believers. This prompted Paul to write a letter to the congregation to encourage them in their faith as well as to address some issues of false teaching that Epaphras brought to his attention. Paul wrote to these Gentile believers:

> *In Him you were also circumcised with a circumcision done not by hand, in the stripping away of the body of the flesh through the circumcision of Messiah. You were buried along with Him in immersion, through which you also were raised with Him by trusting in the working of God, who raised Him from the dead.*
> —**Colossians 2:11–12**

Many children born to Christian parents, especially prior to the Protestant Reformation, were baptized in infancy. If the old covenant had been done away with and circumcision was the sign of that covenant, the reasoning went, then baptism was the sign of the covenant that God had made with Gentile Christians. Infants were circumcised under the old covenant; therefore, the logic was, they were to be baptized under the new. Circumcision was replaced by infant baptism. The replacement came because the early church fathers felt they had to replace everything Jewish. A biblical rite for Jewish people was replaced with a non-biblical tradition.

The problem is that Paul never said any of that. During his time, people were going around to Colossae and other cities where Gentiles had heard the gospel and telling these Gentile believers that they needed to be circumcised in order to be saved. The followers of Yeshua, however, made His stance clear: Gentiles only needed to be immersed, and Jews would continue to circumcise their sons on the eighth day and be immersed in water for the forgiveness of their sins.

Circumcision Is of the Heart

One difference between Jews and Gentiles is that Jews, because of the covenant with Abraham, circumcise our sons on the eighth day and are immersed in water, while Gentiles are immersed in water after they receive Yeshua as their Messiah so they can identify with God's promises throughout Scripture.

Paul was simply saying to the Gentile believers in Colossae, "Don't listen to these guys who are telling you that you have to be circumcised, because you *were* circumcised. It's just that it's a spiritual circumcision, not a circumcision of the flesh."

In Romans 2:29, Paul further clarified that "circumcision is of the heart." This is not a concept that originated in the New Testament, either. Check out Deuteronomy 10:16: "Circumcise the foreskin of your heart therefore, and do not be stiff-necked anymore." The concept of circumcision of the heart was explained further, later in Deuteronomy, after Moses described the blessings Israel would receive for following the covenants and the curses they would receive if they did not follow the covenants:

> *Now when all these things come upon you—the blessing and the curse that I have set before you—and you take them to heart in all the nations where ADONAI your God has banished you, and you return to ADONAI your God and listen to*

> *His voice according to all that I am commanding you to-*
> *day—you and your children—with all your heart and with*
> *all your soul, then ADONAI your God will bring you back*
> *from captivity and have compassion on you, and He will re-*
> *turn and gather you from all the peoples where ADONAI your*
> *God has scattered you. Even if your outcasts are at the ends*
> *of the heavens, from there ADONAI your God will gather you,*
> *and from there He will bring you. ADONAI your God will*
> *bring you into the land that your fathers possessed, and you*
> *will possess it; and He will do you good and multiply you*
> *more than your fathers. Also ADONAI your God will circum-*
> *cise your heart and the heart of your descendants—to love*
> *ADONAI your God with all your heart and with all your soul,*
> *in order that you may live.*
>
> **—Deuteronomy 30:1–6**

So, there's a physical circumcision that Jewish boys have on the eighth day after they are born, and it is a sign of the covenant that God made with Abraham, that He would bless Abraham's physical descendants. When our sons are circumcised and their blood is spilled, they become a part of this covenant.

Moses himself, however, told the Jewish people that unless your circumcision is of the heart, your physical circumcision means nothing. You cannot will yourself to love the Lord your God with all your heart, with all your soul, and with all your strength. It's impossible unless God does a work within you and circumcises your heart.

Paul was saying the same thing back in Colossians, explaining that since God had circumcised the hearts of these Gentile believers, they didn't have to worry about physical circumcision. They had been immersed into Yeshua's death and into His resurrection. When we immerse people in water, the immersion part represents associating yourself with Yeshua's death. Coming back up from the water represents participating in His resurrection.

Immersed into Death and Raised into Life

For Jews and Gentiles alike, God circumcises our hearts so we can love Him with all our heart, with all our soul, and with all our strength. In that moment when you commit to being immersed in water, you are asking God to put you to death so that He can bring you back to life, just like Yeshua was alive, put to death, and in the ground for three days. (Don't worry—that doesn't mean you have to stay underwater for three days!)

Yeshua then came back to life in what we understand as His bodily resurrection. Physically, His body was dead, and then the Holy Spirit breathed life back into Him. The same Spirit who brought Yeshua back from the dead dwells in us:

> But if Messiah is in you, though the body is dead because of sin, yet the Spirit is alive because of righteousness. And if the Ruach of the One who raised Yeshua from the dead dwells in you, the One who raised Messiah Yeshua from the dead will also give life to your mortal bodies through His Ruach who dwells in you.
> *—Romans 8:10–11*

When you allow God to circumcise your heart, you can then experience the death in being immersed in water and the life that comes afterward, because Yeshua was dead and then came back to life. You can have that same life, but God wants to put some things to death. He wants to put to death the sin that is in your life. He wants to put to death your shame and guilt.

This is what circumcision is about for Jewish children when we invite them into the covenant that God made with Abraham, and it is what we have experienced as adults. After we believe that Yeshua is the Messiah, we commit to be immersed in water so that we can experience death and be brought back to life. This is why John the Baptist said, when his disciples were arguing with a Judean over purification, "He must increase, while I must decrease" (John 3:30).

You have to give over the things that are holding you back from following Yeshua with all your heart, with all your soul, and with all your strength. By doing this, He increases in your life and you decrease. You start to understand yourself the way He does and view yourself the way He views you—not the way you view yourself in your own head or the way your parents told you how you should be.

If you believe in Yeshua, the Holy Spirit who raised Him from the dead dwells in you and will help you to see and hear what the Lord is doing. But this means you will have to surrender a whole lot of things that you don't want to surrender. It means you have to ask the Lord to circumcise your heart.

If you're Jewish and you were circumcised on the eighth day, it doesn't mean anything in the end if you don't circumcise your heart. That's not just the New Testament—that's Moses. That's the Torah. Yeshua was perfectly in step with the things that came before Him.

Your circumcision needs to be of the heart, and you can't do that yourself, because it's not done with physical hands. It's done by the power of the Spirit of God. If you ask Him to circumcise your heart, He will, which means He will cut out all the things that don't belong there. He cuts out the darkness, the guilt, the shame, and the pain. He renews your heart and calls you back to Himself.

This is what God has been doing for everyone since the moment He created the heavens and the earth. He has been calling His creation back to Himself, and you are part of that creation.

God is calling you back whether you are a Jewish person who has yet to receive Yeshua as the Messiah or you're a Gentile who needs the Holy Spirit to circumcise your heart. He formed both groups in our mothers' wombs, creating us so we could worship Him in Spirit and in truth.

Decreasing So He May Increase

My prayer for you is that you would decrease so the Lord can increase—that you would ask the Lord to circumcise your heart and to help you understand the things you really want to understand. Allow the Lord to speak into those things. You need to push aside the things you're holding onto so tightly and ask Him to help you let them go so He can increase in your life and the power of the Holy Spirit that raised Yeshua from the dead can do the same thing in you.

The Lord is trying to put you to death, but you may argue with Him. You don't want to give up this or that. You don't want to change your attitude or change your life. You've lived with the frustrations, the shame, and the guilt for so long, you're not sure you can live without them. You're afraid that once you give those things up, God might not really fill you with His Holy Spirit and give you what you need.

God, however, simply encourages you to trust that He has been in everything that's happened in your life up to this point and that it has all been leading you to surrender yourself. He encourages you to allow Him to circumcise your heart.

CONCLUSION

A Continuation

I hope you've enjoyed our adventure together as we've explored the original Jewish context of Yeshua, His disciples, and the New Testament. I hope this has added to your understanding of Yeshua as Messiah, who came first for His Jewish people and also for people from every nation. I hope it's enhanced the joy of your salvation in Him!

In college, I wrote a paper in Theology 101 on circumcision called, "Should Jewish Followers of Yeshua Stop Circumcising Our Children Just Because It Hurts?" My conclusion in the paper was that Jewish followers of Yeshua should continue to circumcise on the eighth day because it was commanded for the physical descendants of Abraham forever while Gentile Christians do not, nor did they ever, share the same obligation. The command comes from Genesis 17:13–14: "Whether born in your household or bought with your money, they must be circumcised. My covenant in your flesh is to be an everlasting covenant. Any uncircumcised male, who has not been circumcised in the flesh, will be cut off from his people; he has broken my covenant."

My professor, who had taught theology for over fifty years, wrote that he was concerned "I was headed towards the heresy of Judaizing." As a novice, I found the word *Judaize* in the Merriam-Webster dictionary and found a simple definition: "to make Jewish."[125] I sat with my professor—whom I learned so much from and honor in my theology even today—for hours. I shared the definition with him and asked a simple question: "If the definition of *Judaize* is 'to make Jewish,' is it even possible to Judaize Jewish people?" He wasn't sure.

I remain positive that it is not possible to Judaize Jews. I get it. For lots of reasons—too great to cover in this book—there is fear for many Christians of moving backwards to Judaism. I am not telling Christians to move backwards, or even encouraging them to make up for two thousand years of history. I am certainly not attempting to turn Christians into Jewish converts who observe Judaism.

I am hopeful, now more than ever, that we are approaching a day when the larger body of Messiah (the Church) will recognize that Jewish people can and should practice Judaism as followers of the Jewish Messiah, Yeshua. I am hopeful the Body will recognize that following Yeshua is the most Jewish decision any Jewish person can make and that when Gentiles turn to God, they turn to the God of Israel in the person of Yeshua.

My goal is not for everyone to keep the Torah but for everyone—both Jews and Gentiles—to see the New Testament as a Jewish book, a part of the Hebrew Scriptures. When David H. Stern finished his work on the Complete Jewish Bible, he pulled a few revolutionary moves. First, he took out the title pages for the Old Testament and the New Testament. In most Christian Bibles, the Old Testament finishes with Malachi.

Then there's a title page that simply reads, "New Testament," and things start fresh with the Gospel of Matthew. There is a clear separation between the "old" and the "new." In the Complete Jewish Bible—and now in the newer Messianic translation, the Tree of Life version—there is no separation. The Bible continues from one book to another.

Second, Stern put the order of the Tanakh back into the Jewish order. The Tanakh, which is also referred to as the Hebrew Bible or the Old Testament, is divided into three sections: the Torah (the five books of Moses), the Nevi'im (the Prophets),[126] and the Ketuvim (the Writings).[127] The name Tanakh comes from the acronym for these three sections, TNK. In Messianic Jewish translations of the Bible, there is no separation between the last book of the Tanakh, which is 2 Chronicles, and the first book of the New Testament, the Gospel of Matthew.

It's not the telling of two stories that are loosely connected. It's all one story designed to bring everyone, Jews and Gentiles, back to the God of Israel. The Tanakh is not just a bunch of stories that point to Jesus. It is a history of the Jewish people and a record of God's promises and their fulfillment. The New Testament continues that same theme, further demonstrating God's faithfulness. What proves God's faithfulness more than sending His promised Messiah to the children of Israel, the Jewish people? It's all that we hoped for, and He came through!

The Jewish Foundation of "the Church"

The narrative common within evangelical Christianity is that God moved among the people of Israel in the Old Testament. He then started the church and Christianity in Acts 2 and began moving in a different direction, away from Judaism. Pastors have to jump through all kinds of hoops to justify this perspective, and it has created much confusion for both Christians and Jews.

In Acts 2, as stated earlier, Yeshua's disciples were celebrating Shavuot. Even the *Jewish Encyclopedia* sees the connection between the festival Shavuot and what has become the Christian celebration of Pentecost. They write, "The relation of the Jewish Shavuot to the Christian Pentecost with its pouring out of the spirit as an analogy to the giving the Law in seventy languages is obvious."[128]

The Gospels present Yeshua's death and resurrection in the context of Passover. Luke presented Acts 2 in the context of Shavuot, just fifty days after Yeshua's resurrection, when he wrote, "To them He showed Himself to be alive after His suffering through many convincing proofs, appearing to them for forty days and speaking about the kingdom of God" (Acts 1:3), and "when the day of Shavuot had come, they were all together in one place" (Acts 2:1).

When Luke pointed out "forty days" in Acts 1 and "Shavuot" in Acts 2, he was referencing what is known in Judaism as "the counting of the Omer." Leviticus 23:16 commands us to count fifty days from the start of Passover to the day of Shavuot. Shavuot is known as the day of first fruits, as we bring a tithe of grain from the first harvest in the fall.

Understanding these days in the Jewish and historical context is crucial to understanding what happened in the Book of Acts. Everything that happened to the disciples in the first two chapters of Acts happened in the context of Passover, the fifty days of Omer, and Shavuot. Knowing this changes our understanding of these events from something random and new to something that was planned out and appointed in Jewish time.

The spread of the gospel to the Gentile world took anywhere from ten to twenty years, depending on the various theories of the timeline of the book of Acts. Again, in the first third of the book of Acts, the story is almost exclusively about the Holy Spirit falling on Jewish followers of Yeshua. The majority of the men present at what is commonly known as "the start of the church" or "the giving of the Holy Spirit" in Acts 2 were Jewish. Luke wrote, "Now Jewish people were staying in Jerusalem, devout men from every nation under heaven" (Acts 2:5). This was made clear in Peter's sermon as he referred to his audience as "Fellow Judeans" (Acts 2:14), "Men of Israel" (Acts 2:22), and "Brothers" (Acts 2:29). He then closed his sermon by saying, "Therefore let the whole house of Israel know for certain that God has made Him—this Yeshua whom you had crucified—both Lord and Messiah!" (Acts 2:36).

Peter is the main focus of Acts 2–5. Acts 6–7 records the testimony and execution of Stephen, one of Yeshua's early followers. It's not until the end of Acts 7 that readers are introduced to Saul, also called Paul. Acts chapters 8–14 go back and forth between Paul and Peter until both men were at the Jerusalem council in Acts 15.

The rest of the book of Acts follows Paul and the spreading of the gospel to Jews and Gentiles all over the known world. Because Paul and Peter were so central to the days and years following Yeshua's ascension, Luke focused on them to show the Jewish foundation of "the church" as an extension and expansion of the Jewish people to include Gentiles who call on the name of Yeshua as members of the family of God.

We Live in Incredible Times

The more simple, wonderful story of the Bible is that God never stops calling people back to Himself, whether they be Jew or Gentile. People sometimes ask the question, "If you could choose any time period to be alive, which one would you choose?" For me, the time we live in right now is the most exciting because we're seeing God do incredible things among Israel, the Jewish people, and we're seeing Him do equally incredible things among the nations, the Gentiles.

We live in an amazing time when Jewish people are turning to Yeshua in Messianic synagogues and churches. At the same time, Gentiles are continuing to come to faith in the Jewish Messiah, and pastors and church members are coming to understand the Jewish context of Yeshua and His disciples.

My answer never changes—I choose right now!

The Jewish Jesus

You can't say you love Jesus and hate Jewish people.

You can't say you love Jesus and view Judaism as legalistic.

You can't say you love Jesus and leave Judaism in the past.

You can't say you love Jesus and tell Jewish people to stop being Jews.

You can't say you love Jesus and say the church > Israel.

You can't say you love Jesus and say Christianity > Judaism.

You can't say you love Jesus and say the New Testament > the Old Testament.

You can't say you love Jesus and say the Gospels > the Torah.

You can't say you love Jesus and hate the Torah.

You can't say you love Jesus and say Easter > Passover.

You can't say you love Jesus and ignore His Jewishness.

You can't say you love Jesus and ignore His practice of Judaism.

You can't say you love Jesus and ignore His Jewish voice to a Jewish world.

You can't say you love Jesus and not see the gospel as a Jewish message.

You can't say you love Jesus and not preach the Jewish gospel to Jewish people.

Jesus is not a Christian.

Jesus is not white.

Jesus is not black.

Jesus is not Palestinian.

Jesus is not a refugee.

Jesus is not an immigrant.

Jesus is not a policy.

Jesus is not your political party.

Jesus is not an American.

Jesus is not a nationalist.

Jesus is not like you.

Jesus does not fit into your image.

Jesus is Jewish.

Jesus is the Torah.

Jesus is the gospel.

Jesus is the hope of the Jewish people.

Jesus is the hope of the Gentile world.

Jesus is the image from which humankind was formed.

Jesus is for the whole world.

Jesus is the way, the truth, and the life.

Jesus is Yeshua.

Yeshua means "salvation" for anyone who calls on His name—for the Jewish people first, and also for Gentiles.

Acknowledgments

To my wife, Laura: There is no end to my love for you or my gratefulness to God that He answered all my prayers in giving you to me. For all the tears, heartache, pain, love, joy, and fun we've had so far—I love you no matter what!

To my children, Emma, Siri, and Ty: My prayer for you is that you fall in love with Yeshua and continue to grow in your understanding of how much He loves you. You three are the greatest joy in my life.

To my parents, David and Helene Rosenberg: I am forever grateful to you for raising me to love the God of my Fathers and Mothers. Who would have thought that this wild ADHD kid would find focus enough to write a book!

To my brothers Jake and Avi and their families: Thank you for being my first friends and audience.

To my sister-in-law Heather: Thank you for helping me flesh out my ideas and for reading what I write.

To my friends Eric McAdams and Troy Wallace: You are both a safe place for me to be me. There's no way I can thank you enough for loving me as I am.

Several leaders have spurred me to press on and continue growing in my walk with God and my own spiritual life: David McQueen, Brad Barshaw, Chris Manginelli, Aaron Gray,

Shawn Hennessey, Wayne Wilks, Tim Ross, Preston Morrison, Jonathan Bernis, and Kevin Solomon, I really couldn't have done this without each of you and your support and investment in me.

To the members and regular attendees of Restoration in Seattle: I can't thank you enough for continuing to follow me as things have changed during my time in Seattle. Moving from a small fellowship of Yeshua followers to a fully functioning synagogue and community has been challenging, but it's been worth every hardship and joy. Thank you for allowing me to grow as a leader while also teaching me how to lead.

I am grateful to our board and leaders for giving me the time to write this book. Thank you to Paul Stein for believing in me first and supporting me as you gave me the keys to your work; to P.K. White for sticking it out and always speaking truthfully; to Wendy White for taking such good care of our family and loving us well; to Kelly Uckun for taking us to the next level professionally and organizationally; to Emily Kennedy for setting up our office and taking care of so many details; to Janet Cothrell for staying on for the ride and offering sound advice; to Matt and Katrina Gile for your friendship and for proof that what we are doing is worth it as long as God is transforming families like yours; I am grateful to serve alongside amazing young leaders who inspire me often like Justin and Rheanne Gloyd, Isaac and Danielle D'Auria, and Shawna Um; and to Aybars Uckun for your faithful friendship and for pushing me to greater things. You are like a brother to me, and I am so glad you are in my daily life!

I stand on the shoulders of men like David H. Stern, translator of the Complete Jewish Bible and author of the foundational books *Messianic Judaism* and the *Jewish New Testament*

Commentary. I am not sure what my identity would look like today without your books!

To Boaz Michael and the staff of First Fruits of Zion in Jerusalem: Thank you for offering not only a place to write but also intellectual stimulation and access to so many resources, authors, and quotes in the David H. Stern Library at the Bram Center.

To Brayden Brookshier and the team at Sermon To Book: Thank you for your partnership in this work. It was a wonderful experience, and I'm grateful for you and your team.

To Jewish Voice Ministries International, Jewish Ministry at Gateway Church (Dallas), Troy and Jen Wallace, and Restoration in Seattle: Thank you for investing in this work. Your faith in me keeps pushing me forward.

REFERENCES

Notes

1. *BibliaTodo Dictionary,* "Sukkot." https://www.bibliatodo.com/en/bible-dictionary/sukkot.

2. FFOZ Israel Staff. "The Season of Our Joy." *First Fruits of Zion.* October 8, 2014. https://ffoz.org/discover/jewish-holidays/the-season-of-our-joy.html.

3. Donner, Richard, dir. *The Goonies.* Warner Bros, 1985.

4. *BibliaTodo Dictionary,* "kippah-key-pah." https://www.bibliatodo.com/en/bible-dictionary/kippah-key-puh.

5. *BibliaTodo Dictionary,* "tzitzit." https://www.bibliatodo.com/en/bible-dictionary/tzitzit.

6. *BibliaTodo Dictionary,* "Yeshuah." https://www.bibliatodo.com/en/bible-dictionary/yeshuah.

7. *BibliaTodo Dictionary,* "Shabbat." https://www.bibliatodo.com/en/bible-dictionary/shabbat.

8. *BibliaTodo Dictionary,* "Yosef." https://www.bibliatodo.com/en/bible-dictionary/yosef.

9. *BibliaTodo Dictionary*, "Eretz-yisrael." https://www.bibliatodo.com/en/bible-dictionary/eretz-yisrael.

10. Boteach, Shmuley. *Kosher Jesus*. Gefen Publishing House, 2012, p. ix–x.

11. Falcon, Ted, and David Blatner. *Judaism for Dummies*. John Wiley & Sons, 2018, p. 21.

12. Falcon, *Judaism*, p. 372.

13. Boyarin, Daniel. *The Jewish Gospels: The Story of the Jewish Christ*. New Press/ORIM, 2012, p. 104.

14. "The Letter of Rabbi Jacob Emden." In *Jesus Beyond Christianity: The Classic Texts*. Edited by Gregory A. Barker and Stephen E. Gregg. Oxford University Press, 2010, p. 30.

15. Benamozegh, Elia. *Israel and Humanity*. Paulist Press, 1995, p. 329–330.

16. Briggs, Kenneth A. "Jewish Scholars Reassessing Biblical Jesus." *The New York Times*. February 2, 1978. https://www.nytimes.com/1978/02/02/archives/new-jersey-pages-jewish-scholars-reassessing-historical-jesus.html.

17. Lapide, Pinchas. *Jesus in Two Perspectives: A Jewish-Christian Dialogue*. Augsburg Publishing House, 1985, p. 114.

18. I am indebted to lists of Jewish opinions of Jesus created by Jews for Jesus: https://jewsforjesus.org/answers/some-jewish-views-of-jesus-2/.

19. Cousins, Norman. Quoted in Jonathan Bernis, *A Rabbi Looks at Jesus of Nazareth*. Chosen Books, 2011, p. 229.

20. Maimonides. "Mishneh Torah." *Hilkhot Melakhim* (XI, 4). Cited by Pinchas Lapide, *The Resurrection of Jesus: A Jewish Perspective*. Augsburg Publishing House, 1983, p. 143.

21. Poljak, Abram. *The Cross in the Star of David*. Jewish Christian Community Press, 1938, p. 50.

22. *BibliaTodo Dictionary*, "haftarah-hahf-toh- ruh." https://www.bibliatodo.com/en/bible-dictionary/haftarah-hahf-toh-ruh.

23. *BibliaTodo Dictionary*, "sukkah." https://www.bibliatodo.com/en/bible-dictionary/sukkah.

24. *BibliaTodo Dictionary*, "bar-mitzvah." https://www.bibliatodo.com/en/bible-dictionary/bar-mitzvah.

25. *BibliaTodo Dictionary*, "Tanakh-tuhn-ahkh." https://www.bibliatodo.com/en/bible-dictionary/tanakh-tuhn-ahkh.

26. *BibliaTodo Dictionary*, "goy naval." https://www.bibliatodo.com/en/bible-dictionary/goy-naval.

27. *BibliaTodo Dictionary*, "Gentile." https://www.bibliatodo.com/en/bible-dictionary/gentile.

28. Stanley, Andy. *Irresistible: Reclaiming the New That Jesus Unleashed for the World.* Zondervan, 2018, p. 20.

29. Stanley, *Irresistible*, p. 123.

30. Enelow, Hyman G. "A Jewish View of Jesus." In *Selected Works of Hyman G. Enelow, Volume III: Collected Writings.* Privately printed, 1935, p. 441–442, 509. Quoted in "Some Jewish Views of Jesus." June 30, 2011. Jews for Jesus. https://jewsforjesus.org/answers/some-jewish-views-of-jesus-2.

31. Manning, Brennan. *The Signature of Jesus.* Crown Publishing Group, 2011, p. 37–38.

32. Varriano, John. "At Supper with Leonardo." *Gastronomica: The Journal for Food Studies.* February 10, 2008. https://gastronomica.org/2008/02/10/at-supper-leonardo/.

33. Hecht, Mendy. "The 613 Commandments (Mitzvot)." Chabad-Lubavitch Media Center. https://www.chabad.org/library/article_cdo/aid/756399/jewish/The-613-Commandments-Mitzvot.htm.

34. Tozer, A. W. *The Pursuit of God.* Christian Publications, 1948.

35. The Tetragrammaton, referred to in rabbinic literature as HaShem (The Name) or Shem Hameforash (The Special Name), is the word used to refer to the four-letter word *yud-hey-vav-hey* (יהוה) that is the name for God used in the Hebrew Bible. Some attempts to pronounce the word are *Yahweh* and *Jehovah*.

36. "What Is the Tetragrammaton? The Unpronounceable Name of God." MyJewishLearning.com. https://www.myjewishlearning.com/article/the-tetragrammaton/.

37. *BibliaTodo Dictionary*, "Shavuot." https://www.bibliatodo.com/en/bible-dictionary/shavuot.

38. Johnston, Joe, dir. *Honey, I Shrunk the Kids*. Buena Vista Pictures, 1989.

39. Josephus, Flavius. "Antiquities of the Jews" 17.2.4. *The Genuine Works of Flavius Josephus the Jewish Historian*. Translated by William Whiston. 1737. https://penelope.uchicago.edu/josephus/ant-17.html.

40. For more information on the historical outline of Talmudic Judaism, visit: https://people.ucalgary.ca/~elsegal/RelS367/RabbinicTimeline.html.

41. Boyarin, *The Jewish Gospels,* p. 104.

42. *BibliaTodo Dictionary*, "Yom-Kippur." https://www.bibliatodo.com/en/bible-dictionary/yom-kippur.

43. "Every Jot and Tittle Is Important." *Torah Portions*. First Fruits of Zion. https://torahportions.ffoz.org/disciples/matthew/every-jot-and-tittle-is-import.html.

44. Rosenberg, David. "The Word As a Way of Life." Shuvah Yisrael Messianic Synagogue. http://shuvah.com/word-as-a-way-of-life.

45. "Worship Services: V'ahavta (Read)." Reform Judaism. https://reformjudaism.org/practice/prayers-blessings/worship-services-vahavta-read.

46. *BibliaTodo Dictionary*, "shema." https://www.bibliatodo.com/en/bible-dictionary/shema.

47. *BibliaTodo Dictionary,* "kadosh." https://www.bibliatodo.com/en/bible-dictionary/kadosh.

48. The JPS commentary on Numbers says (p. 410–411): "In the ancient near east ... the hem was ornate in comparison with the rest of the robe. The more important the individual the more elaborate the embroidery of his hem ... an extension of its owner's person and authority."

49. JPS commentary (p. 127): "The violet, or blue-purple, dye was extracted from the gland of the Murex trunculus snail found in shallow waters off the coast of norther Israel and Lebanon. Since it has been shown that 12,000 snails yield only 1.4 grams of dye, it can be readily understood why only royalty could afford it; and hence the term "royal blue or purple."

50. "Tekhelet: The Mystery of the Long-Lost Biblical Blue Thread." Chabad-Lubavitch Media Center. https://www.chabad.org/library/article_cdo/aid/530 127/jewish/Tekhelet-The-Mystery-of-the-Long-Lost-Biblical-Blue-Thread. htm.

51 . Kaplan, Aryeh. "All About the Messiah." Aish HaTorah. https://www.aish.com/jl/li/m/48944241.html.

52 . *BibliaTodo Dictionary,* "raca." https://www.bibliatodo.com/en/bible-dictionary/raca.

53. *BibliaTodo Dictionary,* "gehenna." https://www.bibliatodo.com/en/bible -dictionary/gehenna.

54. Lucas, George, dir. *Star Wars: The Phantom Menace.* Lucasfilm, 1999.

55. Dobov, Nissan Dovid. "Chapter 7: Hillel and Rabbi Akiva." Chabad-Lubavitch Media Center. https://www.chabad.org/library/article_cdo/aid/231 2343/jewish/Chapter-7-Hillel-and-Rabbi-Akiva.htm.

56. Boyarin, *The Jewish Gospels*, p. 104.

57. The only author in question in terms of Jewishness is Luke. Until recently, most believed he was a Gentile. Interestingly, in the New Testament, Luke and Acts are among the most Jewish in terms of content.

58. Stanley, *Irresistible*, p.133–134.

59. Stanley, *Irresistible*, p. 135.

60. Stanley, *Irresistible*, p. 52–53.

61. Stanley, *Irresistible*, p. 54.

62. *BibliaTodo Dictionary,* "kohanim." https://www.bibliatodo.com/en/bible -dictionary/kohanim.

63. *Encyclopaedia Britannica,* "Samaritan." https://www.britannica.com/ topic/Samaritan.

64. Heschel, Abraham. Quoted in Danah Zohar and Ian Marshall, *SQ: Connecting with Our Spiritual Intelligence.* Bloomsbury Publishing USA, 2000, p. 15.

65. Freud, Sigmund. *The Future of an Illusion.* L. & Virginia Woolf at the Hogarth Press and the Institute of Psycho-Analysis, 1928.

66. Orwell, George. "Politics and the English Language." In *Shooting an Elephant and Other Essays.* Secker and Warburg, 1950.

67. Higgins, Julissa. "Read George W. Bush's Speech at the Dallas Shooting Memorial Service." Time. July 12, 2016. https://time.com/ 4403510/george-w-bush-speech-dallas-shooting-memorial-service/.

68. Eisenberg, Ronald L. *The 613 Mitzvot: A Contemporary Guide to the Commandments of Judaism.* Schreiber, 2001.

69. *BibliaTodo Dictionary,* "kosher." https://www.bibliatodo.com/en/bible-dictionary/kosher.

70. Stanley, Andy. "Follow." Study Gateway. HarperCollins Christian Publishing. https://www.studygateway.com/watch/follow.

71. Schaeffer, Francis. *The God Who Is There.* InterVarsity Press, 2020, p. 50.

72. McNeill, Donald P., Douglas A. Morrison, and Henri J. Nouwen. *Compassion: A Reflection on the Christian Life.* Image Books/Doubleday, 2006, p. 3–4.

73. Biblical Archaeology Society. "The Bethesda Pool, Site of One of Jesus' Miracles." Bible History Daily. January 18, 2020. https://www.biblicalarch aeology.org/daily/biblical-sites-places/jerusalem/the-bethesda-pool-site-of-one-of-jesus-miracles/.

74. *BibliaTodo Dictionary,* "ruach." https://www.bibliatodo.com/en/bible-dictionary/ruach.

75. Byrne, Joseph Patrick. "Anti-Semitism and Anti-Jewish Violence Before the Black Death." *Encyclopedia of the Black Death.* Vol. 1. ABC-CLIO, 2012, p. 15.

76. Pasachoff, Naomi E., and Robert J. Littman. *A Concise History of the Jewish People.* Rowman & Littlefield, 2005, p. 154.

77. MyJewishLearning.com. "Ritual Hand Washing Before Meals: The Netilat Yadayim Practice and Blessing." https://www.myjewishlearning.com /article/hand-washing/.

78. MJL. "Ritual Hand Washing Before Meals: The Netilat Yadayim Practice and Blessing." MyJewishLearning.com. https://www.myjewishlearning.com /article/hand-washing/.

79. Stanley, "Follow."

80. Stern, David H. *Restoring the Jewishness of the Gospel: A Message for Christians Condensed from Messianic Judaism.* Messianic Jewish Publishers, 2009.

81. Michaels, D. "Jews Should Now Be Able to Accept New View of Jesus." Jewish Exponent. January 30, 2013. https://www.jewishexponent.com/2013/ 01/30/jews-should-now-be-able-to-accept-new-view-of-jesus/.

82. "11 Facts About the Holocaust." DoSomething.org. https://www. do something.org/us/facts/11-facts-about-holocaust.

83. Catholic Church. "283. What Is the Meaning of *Transubstantiation?*" In *Compendium of Catechism of the Catholic Church.* USCCB Publishing, 2006, p. 84.

84. *Encyclopaedia Britannica,* "consubstantiation." https://www.britannica.com/topic/consubstantiation.

85. Mathison, Keith. "Calvin's Doctrine of the Lord's Supper." Ligonier Ministries. https://www.ligonier.org/learn/articles/calvins-doctrine-lords-supper/.

86. "Five Views of the Eucharist." Christianity in View. 2016. http://christianityinview.com/eucharist.html.

87. "New Testament Timeline." ESV Study Bible Online. Crossway. https://www.esv.org/resources/esv-global-study-bible/chart-40-00-nt-timeline/.

88. *BibliaTodo Dictionary,* "kiddush." https://www.bibliatodo.com/en/bible-dictionary/kiddush.

89. *BibliaTodo Dictionary,* "hamotzi." https://www.bibliatodo.com/en/bible-dictionary/hamotzi.

90. *BibliaTodo Dictionary,* "havdalah.". https://www.bibliatodo.com/en/bible-dictionary/havdalah.

91. Adler, Cyrus, and Lewis N. Dembitz. "Kiddush." JewishEncyclopedia.com. http://www.jewishencyclopedia.com/articles/9307-kiddush.

92. Jenkins, Michael H. "Bread and Wine As Religious Symbols." Leaf Group. https://classroom.synonym.com/bread-wine-as-religious-symbols-12086673.html.

93. Storms, Sam. "10 Things You Should Know About the Lord's Supper and Communion." Crosswalk. https://www.crosswalk.com/faith/bible-study/10-things-you-should-know-about-the-lord-s-supper-from-1-corinthians.html.

94. *BibliaTodo Dictionary,* "bracha." https://www.bibliatodo.com/en/bible-dictionary/bracha.

95. Shurpin, Yehuda. "Why Is Kiddush Said Over Wine?" Chabad-Lubavitch Media Center. https://www.chabad.org/library/article_cdo/aid/3340700/jewish/Why-Is-Kiddush-Said-Over-Wine.htm#footnote16a3340700.

96. Snyder, B. J. "Baptism." *Lexham Theological Wordbook.* Edited by D. Mangum, D. R. Brown, R. Klippenstein, and R. Hurst. Lexham Press, 2014.

97. Hasson, Nir. "Jerusalem Family Finds 2,000-Year Old Mikveh Underneath Living Room." Haaretz. July 1, 2015. https://www.haaretz.com/archaeology/family-finds-2-000-year-old-mikveh-under-house-1.5374825.

98. Witherington, B., III. *The Acts of the Apostles: A Socio-rhetorical Commentary.* Wm. B. Eerdmans Publishing Co., 1998, p. 347.

99. Barker, Kenneth L., and John R. Kohlenberger. *Zondervan NIV Bible Commentary.* Vol. 2. Zondervan, 1999, p. 462.

100. Ryrie, C. C. *Basic Theology: A Popular Systematic Guide to Understanding Biblical Truth.* Moody Press, 1999, p. 466.

101. Dockery, D. S., ed. *Holman Bible Handbook.* Holman Bible Publishers, 1992, p. 834.

102. Elwell, W. A., and B. J. Beitzel. "Church." *Baker Encyclopedia of the Bible.* Vol. 1. Baker Book House, 1988, p. 461.

103. Millard Erickson, *Christian Theology.* Baker Publishing Group, 1998.

104. BibleProject. "Overview: Acts Ch. 1–12." Youtube video. October 4, 2016. https://www.youtube.com/watch?v=CGbNw855ksw.

105. Manser, Martin H., Alister E. McGrath, J. I. Packer, and Donald J. Wiseman, eds. *Dictionary of Bible Themes: The Accessible and Comprehensive Tool for Topical Studies.* Zondervan, 1999.

106. Fernando, Ajith. *NIV Application Commentary: Acts.* Zondervan Academic, 1998, p. 271.

107. Maiers, B. "Samaritans." *The Lexham Bible Dictionary.* Edited by J. D. Barry, D. Bomar, D. R. Brown, R. Klippenstein, D. Mangum, C. Sinclair Wolcott, and W. Widder. Lexham Press, 2016.

108. Polhill, J. B. *Acts.* Vol. 26. Broadman & Holman Publishers, 1992, p. 255–256.

109. Polhill, *Acts*, p. 258.

110. Woodall, D. L. "Cornelius." *The Lexham Bible Dictionary.* Edited by J. D. Barry, D. Bomar, D. R. Brown, R. Klippenstein, D. Mangum, C. Sinclair Wolcott, and W. Widder. Lexham Press, 2016.

111. Zwick, Joel. *My Big Fat Greek Wedding.* IFC Films, 2002.

112. Stern, D. H. "Acts 10:28." *Jewish New Testament Commentary: A Companion Volume to the Jewish New Testament.* Electronic ed. Jewish New Testament Publications, 1996.

113. Spitzer, Jeffrey. "The Non-Jew in Jewish Law." MyJewishLearning. com. https://www.myjewishlearning.com/article/the-non-jew-in-jewish-law.

114. Wall, Robert, N. T. Wright, and J. Paul Sampley. *The New Interpreter's Bible: Acts, Introduction to Epistolary Literature, Romans, 1 Corinthians.* Vol. 10. Edited by Leander E. Keck. Abingdon Press, 2002, p. 160.

115. Stern, D. H. "Acts 10:28." *Jewish New Testament Commentary: A Companion Volume to the Jewish New Testament.* Electronic ed. Jewish New Testament Publications, 1996.

116. "New Testament Timeline." ESV Study Bible Online. Crossway. https://www.esv.org/resources/esv-global-study-bible/chart-40-00-nt-timeline/.

117. Janicki, Toby. *The Way of Life – Didache: A New Translation and Messianic Jewish Commentary.* Vine of David, 2017, p. 26.

118. Fernando, *NIV Application Commentary,* p. 415.

119. *The William Davidson Talmud,* "Yevamot 46a." The Sefaria Library. https://www.sefaria.org/Yevamot.46a?lang=bi.

120. Barker, Kenneth L., and John R. Kohlenberger, III, eds. *Zondervan NIV Bible Commentary.* Zondervan Publishing House, 1994, p. 462.

121. Holladay, Carl R. *Acts: A Commentary.* Westminster John Knox Press, 2016, p. 302.

122. Holladay, *Acts,* p. 302.

123. Wilson, Mark. "James or Jacob in the Bible?" Biblical Archaeology Society. https://www.biblicalarchaeology.org/daily/biblical-topics/bible-versions-and-translations/james-or-jacob-in-the-bible/.

124. Hoffbrand, David. *The Jewish Jesus: Reconnecting with the Truth About Jesus, Israel, and the Church.* Destiny Image, 2017, p. 193.

125. *Merriam-Webster.com Dictionary,* "Judaize." https://www.merriam-webster.com/dictionary/Judaize.

126. *BibliaTodo Dictionary,* "neviim." https://www.bibliatodo.com/en/bible-dictionary/neviim.

127. *BibliaTodo Dictionary,* "Tanakh-tuhn-ahkh." https://www.bibliatodo.com/en/bible-dictionary/tanakh-tuhn-ahkh.

128. Kohler, Kaufmann, J. L. Magnus, and Judah David Eisenstein. "Pentecost." JewishEncyclopedia.com. www.jewishencyclopedia.com/articles/12012-pentecost.

About the Author

Matt is the Chief Officer of Awesome (COA) and Rabbi of Restoration (ShalomSeattle.com) in Seattle, WA. A second-generation Messianic Jew and Messianic Rabbi, he received a B.A. in Religion from Nyack College. He is a lover of Apple products, sneakers, track jackets, hoodies, and Steven Spielberg movies and has always dreamt of becoming the fifth member of Boyz II Men. Matt is a leader among his generation in the Messianic movement and he serves as a board member of Jewish Voice Ministries International (jvmi.org). Matt and his wife, Laura, have three children and live in Seattle.

About Sermon To Book

SermonToBook.com began with a simple belief: that sermons should be touching lives, *not* collecting dust. That's why we turn sermons into high-quality books that are accessible to people all over the globe.

Turning your sermon series into a book exposes more people to God's Word, better equips you for counseling, accelerates future sermon prep, adds credibility to your ministry, and even helps make ends meet during tight times.

John 21:25 tells us that the world itself couldn't contain the books that would be written about the work of Jesus Christ. Our mission is to try anyway. Because in heaven, there will no longer be a need for sermons or books. Our time is now.

If God so leads you, we'd love to work with you on your sermon or sermon series.

Visit www.sermontobook.com to learn more.

Made in the USA
Coppell, TX
04 September 2022